SENTENCE CPR

Breathing Life Into Sentences That Might As Well Be Pushing Up Daisies

Phyllis Beveridge Nissila

Cottonwood Press, Inc.
Fort Collins, Colorado

Requests for special permission should be addressed to:

Cottonwood Press, Inc.
109-B Cameron Drive
Fort Collins, Colorado 80525

E-mail: cottonwood@cottonwoodpress.com
Web: www.cottonwoodpress.com
Phone: 800-864-4297
Fax: 970-204-0761

ISBN: 978-1-877673-97-9

Printed in the United States of America

To my family and my students,
who continually inspire me with their wit and wisdom

Table of Contents

Part I

WRITING TIPS

For Revitalizing

Dull Sentences

Sometimes all it takes to inject energy into weak writing is a specific detail here, an active verb there. Other times, cutting away needless words or drawing fresh comparisons will cure what ails a sentence or a paragraph.

This section focuses on writing tips that will help cure problems that lead to weak writing. Advice offered in this section:

- Bring sentences to life with **details**.
- Light a fire under tired sentences by using **active voice**.
- Draw attention to what you say with **fresh similes**.
- Perk up sentences by **showing instead of telling**.
- Avoid bloat by eliminating **word overdose**.
- Build strong sentences with **powerful verbs**.
- Lose the ho-hum by using **vivid metaphors**.

Enjoy!

Name _____

Bring Sentences to Life with
DETAILS

Some sentences suffer from "detail deficiency." In other words, the sentences are boring or inadequate because they just don't provide enough information. Here are two examples of sentences that just don't tell us much:

- They saw it.
- It was interesting.

But look at the difference when we add some specific details:

- Ludmilla and Eddy were pretty sure that the talking eel they saw in the subway this morning was the same one they had seen in the deli last week.
- It was the largest, noisiest insect Rodney had seen in his underwear drawer so far.

A good way to think of interesting details is to answer some or all of these questions: *Who? What? When? Where? Why? How?*

WHO are you talking about? Are you talking about Professor Anklebone? Clutch, Wally's pet boa constrictor? The Polka Renegade Band?

WHAT are you talking about? Are you talking about the hairball Fuzzy coughed up? A cement-wad of gray gum under the last desk in the fifth row? The rabbit on the escalator?

WHEN did it happen? Did it happen it yesterday morning right after the baby dumped his oatmeal on the floor? During a slight pause in the accordion solo? The last time Ms. Clementi saw Elvis in the appliance repair shop?

WHERE did it happen? Did it happen in the middle of the school cafeteria after Scooter spilled his creamed corn? On the Screamin' Demon roller coaster right after lunch? Down the hall, behind the second door on the right?

WHY did it happen? Did it happen because Howard forgot he was in public? Because Clutch got loose? Because Maurice forgot to tighten the lug nuts?

HOW did it happen, or HOW did he/she/they react? Did it happen because someone and his large dog apparently missed the "wet paint on floor" sign? Did Chester scream and slide slowly off his chair in shock because Marla accidentally stapled his ear? Did Dr. Axelrod freak when someone dropped a gummy worm into the petri dish?

(continued)

Details *continued*

Here are some examples of ailing sentences that have been revitalized with details.

Before	After
• He laughed.	• Buddy snickered as Lulu recited yet another SpongeBob SquarePants haiku.
• We were glad we rescued him.	• Chrissy, Jimbo and I jumped for joy when we finally freed the gecko from the tub of Cheez Whiz.
• Alvin got a neat job.	• Alvin the Aardvark Whisperer just signed on with the Animal Network.
• He looked at her.	• Franklin peered deeply into Elvira's dark, reflective eyes, hoping he could see if his hairpiece was on straight.
• Mom looked weird.	• Mom's face got all splotchy when she found Carlton's moldy socks stuck to the bottom of his gym bag.

Practice #1. Improve the following sentences by adding any combination of "W" details (*Who? What? Where? When? Why?*) or "H" (*How?*). Use at least two for each sentence—for example, a *Who* and a *How*, or a *When* and a *Where*.

Be sure to replace any general terms with specific names and places.

1. They saw it.
2. He actually drank it.
3. The baby "spoke."
4. It was creepy.
5. They laughed when they saw it.
6. He was scared.
7. She glared at him.
8. They ran.
9. We ate and ate.
10. It moved.

Practice #2. Create five different versions of the following sentence by adding details. Keep the same basic meaning for each sentence, but make the details different for each.

He said.

Light a Fire Under Tired Sentences by Using
ACTIVE VOICE

Imagine a child saying this: "Mom! Your dresser was painted by Freddy, and all your purple fingernail polish was used."

It probably wouldn't happen. Instead, the child would say, "Mom! Freddy painted your dresser and used all your purple fingernail polish!" The child would know instinctively that active voice communicates a lot better than passive voice. Active voice gets up and moves. Passive voice is sluggish and slow.

Okay, what is passive voice? What is active voice?

With active voice, the subject of the sentence is acting or doing something. (*Freddy painted. Freddy is doing something—painting.*) In passive voice, the subject of the sentence is receiving the action. (*The dresser was painted. The dresser isn't doing anything. It is receiving the action.*)

Here are some more examples.

Passive	Active
• It **was discovered** by Francis that the freshness date on the jar of pickled liver was 1982.	• Francis **discovered** that the freshness date on the jar of pickled liver was 1982.
• Clearly, another win for the tap dancing act "Riverdance, High Wire Version" was what **was wanted** by the *Extreme American Idol* crowd.	• Clearly, the *Extreme American Idol* crowd **wanted** the tap dancing act "Riverdance, High Wire Version" to win again.
• The results of the watermelon toss competition **were announced** by Principal Swindlehoffer.	• Principal Swindlehoffer **announced** the results of the watermelon toss competition.

Passive voice is not grammatically incorrect, and sometimes it's the best choice, especially when you don't know who is doing the acting. (Example: *The satellite photos show that a tear in the ozone* **was patched** *with what appears to be duct tape. We don't know who or what apparently used that duct tape, so passive voice makes sense.)*

Generally, though, active voice is much stronger.

(continued)

Practice #1. The sentences below are in passive voice. Rewrite them so that they are in active voice. You will need to change some words around and add or delete words. (Hint: The verbs in bold are the words that must be replaced.)

1. It **is hoped** by Crenshaw that the fungus **is** not **noticed** by Cloris.
2. The stilt-dancing competition **was hosted** by Mortimer P. Windjammer High School for the third year in a row.
3. The kelp and radish soufflé **was made** by Aunt Balista.
4. Making us eat Aunt Balista's soufflé **was regretted** very soon after dinner by Mom.
5. The pan of red paint the puppies had been playing in **was found** quickly by Pietro.

Practice #2. The sentences below are in passive voice. Rewrite them so that they are in active voice. You will need to change some words around and add or delete words. (Hint: In these sentences, the noun that should do the acting is the word in bold. Be sure this word is the subject of the sentence.)

1. Another sleepless night was expected by **Timmy** after watching *Night of the Melting Eyeballs.*
2. Now that Grandpa is in the nursing home, wild boar hunting has been taken up by **Grandma.**
3. A career switch from psychiatry to cage wrestling has just been announced by **Dr. Feldon Bazooka.**
4. Because she will be needing extra money, teaching the "Chicken Dance" on YouTube is being planned by **Aunt Gladdy.**
5. "Why didn't you tell me that this parrot blurts out, 'Whoa! Who stinks?' at random intervals?" the pet store owner was asked by **Mrs. Winthrop Overstreet.**

Practice #3. The sentences below are in passive voice. Rewrite them so that they are in active voice—this time with no hints.

1. A snag in Lord Hemisphere's chainmail was noted by Frederick, the armor designer.
2. Love letters to Hannah Montana's alleged cousin twice removed, Twyla Tennessee, were written by Damian.

Draw Attention to What you Say with
FRESH SIMILES

A simile is a comparison that uses the words "like" or "as." If you write, "The dead rodent Bonzo dragged in from the barn smelled like that moose meat we forgot in the camper all week," you are using a simile. You are comparing the dead rodent to moose meat forgotten in the camper all week, and you are doing it in a way that makes the reader really get a sense of that dead rodent.

Here's another example: "Pete thought the expensive painting entitled 'In the Desert' looked more like 'Explosion of Furballs and Oatmeal,' but he kept this to himself."

Good similes create an impression that helps the reader imagine how something looks, sounds, tastes, feels, or smells. The problem most writers have with similes, however, is that they often think of similes that are clichés: *Quiet as a mouse. Dead as a doornail. Nutty as a fruitcake.* These similes are so overused that they don't help create much of an impression.

Below is a list of common clichés that are also similes. Try to avoid them.

---

loose as a goose • **blind as a bat** • **busy as a bee** • **cold as ice**

pale as a ghost • **like a bull in a china shop** • **light as a feather** • **flat as a pancake**

fight like cats and dogs • **lie like a rug** • **like a kid in a candy store** • **easy as pie**

avoid like the plague • **mad as a hornet** • **sick as a dog** • **good as gold**

cry like a baby • **sell like hotcakes** • **as pleased as punch** • **eat like a pig**

flat as a board • **white as a ghost** • **shake like a leaf** • **strong as an ox**

hungry as a bear • **pretty as a picture** • **cool as a cucumber**

Here are three ways to create more original, interesting similes:

• Make the comparison more specific. Instead of *as busy as bees,* try *as busy as bees on a pollen mission* or *as busy as bees on a honey deadline* or *busy as bees trying to swarm in a wind tunnel.*

• Exchange the existing verbs or nouns with more specific ones. Instead of *fighting like cats and dogs,* consider *fighting like Chihuahuas in a tote* or *fighting like tomcats in a Dumpster.*

• Think of something entirely new for the comparison. Instead of *mad as a hornet,* try *mad as a cat in a bubblebath.* Instead of *flat as a board,* consider *flat as day-old roadkill.*

(continued)

Practice #1. The similes in the sentences below are all clichés. Replace the clichés with fresh similes. Write your replacement similes on the lines provided.

1. Gwyneth popped her bubble gum for the twenty-seventh time that evening, which is another reason Alfred began *avoiding her like the plague.* _____

   _____

2. Although he felt *like a bull in a china shop,* Bubba promised Wendy he would take the ballet class with her. _____

   _____

3. Keisha changed the oil in the cement truck for her boyfriend, who thought she was *as sweet as pie* to do that.

   _____

   _____

4. When she saw what her three-year-old had done with old shoe polish he found in a box in the cupboard, Eva *cried like a baby.* _____

   _____

5. "I will NOT sit near you!" Tricia said to Buddy. "You're eating *like a pig.*"

   _____

   _____

6. Little Timmy looked *as pale as a ghost* after viewing the Weird Science Network special on those little bugs that can crawl right through your eardrum and lay their eggs in your brain while you sleep. _____

   _____

Practice #2. Write two sentences that include similes. Topic ideas: *What happened when Bubba attended ballet class with Wendy? What else scares little Timmy?* Or choose a subject of your own.

Name _____

Breathe Life into These
YAWNERS

Practice #1. You have learned that you can make sentences more interesting and effective by adding details, using active voice, and writing fresh similes. Review what you have learned by using these techniques to improve the sentences below. (You don't have to use all three techniques with each sentence. Mix and match.)

1. It was a nice vacation except for that.

2. He was as sick as a dog after he ate the casserole.

3. The baseball was hit pretty far.

4. The carnival ride was fun.

5. She was surprised by the noise.

Practice #2. Rewrite the following story, improving it by adding details, using active voice, and writing fresh similes.

Surprisingly, Maria was as cool as a cucumber when it was announced by Anderson that he was calling off their engagement. Later, when it hit her, she was as mad as a hornet—a really big one. The flowers, the wedding cake, and the invitations had already been ordered by her mother. The band had been booked months ago. After thinking it over, Maria decided to have a party anyway. The only thing missing would be Anderson.

(continued)

Name _____

Breathe Life into These
YAWNERS

Practice. Write a short paragraph of at least three sentences about each topic below. Be sure all the sentences are in active voice and include plenty of details. Use similes in at least three of the sentences.

1. Write about Kim's first music lesson.

2. Write about the problems of Contestant #42 in the cooking competition.

3. Write about Ralph getting lost on the first day of school.

4. Write about the animal on the bus.

Perk Up Sentences by
SHOWING Instead of TELLING

Many a reader has nodded off reading sentence after sentence like the following:

- It was a boring program.

- Lester is weird.

It is often much more effective to describe an action that lets us figure out for ourselves that the program was boring or that Lester is weird. In other words, *showing* is usually better than *telling*.

The following sentences are much more interesting because they let us draw our own conclusions:

- Several of us in the front row fell asleep and slid off our chairs at the Pan Flute Festival. (*We can conclude for ourselves that it was boring.*)

- Lester juggled his collection of porcelain rodents. (*Who juggles porcelain rodents? We can figure out for ourselves that Lester is a strange guy.*)

Here are some more examples of showing instead of telling. The "before" sentences *tell*. The "after" sentences *show*.

Before	After
• We were tense.	• When we heard the news that Hector had finally made contact with the Onion Creatures from Jupiter, jaws clenched, stomachs knotted, noses twitched.
• It was a strange conversation.	• "Xgrst?" asked one of the Onion Creatures, to which Hector replied, "It depends."
• We were surprised.	• Although we knew Hector was fluent in twelve languages, including cyber babble, we had no idea he knew Onionese.

(continued)

Practice. Breathe life into the following sentences by showing instead of telling. To help show, use action words. It's also helpful to use sensory words—words that help a reader see, hear, smell, taste, or touch what you are describing.

Example

Before: She doesn't look well.

After: Patch, our gray, white and tan calico, turned green after eating that thing she found under the shed.

1. She is talented. _____

_____

2. We had an odd visitor. _____

_____

3. He is a bad driver. _____

_____

4. She is overly cheerful. _____

_____

5. He is very shy. _____

_____

6. The movie is scary._____

_____

7. He's so cool. _____

_____

8. My dog is smart._____

_____

9. They were tense. _____

_____

10. He was mad . _____

_____

Avoid Bloat by Eliminating
WORD OVERDOSE

Bloated prose is writing that is too wordy. It uses several words when one or two will do. It uses inflated-sounding phrases and empty words.

Study the following examples. The "before" sentences are bloated. The "after" sentences have the same meaning as the original, but they are clearer because they are shorter and simpler.

Before	**After**
• Vladimir *made the announcement of* his promotion to head beet peeler at the soup factory.	• Vladimir *announced* his promotion to head beet peeler at the soup factory.
• *For an additional remittance of $19.99*, we will send you the portable face polisher with your order of a case of Complexion Wow.	• *For $19.99 more*, we will send you the portable face polisher with your order of a case of Complexion Wow.
• Dr. Bazooka said, "*I have come to the conclusion that* Marvin simply prefers living upside down in a cave like a bat."	• Dr. Bazooka said, "*I have concluded that* Marvin simply prefers living upside down in a cave like a bat."
• *In the event that* Mr. Hornsmacker clears his throat and rolls his eyes before handing tests back, you can be pretty sure the class grade point average took a dive.	• *If* Mr. Hornsmacker clears his throat and rolls his eyes before handing tests back, you can be pretty sure the class grade point average took a dive.
• Francesca is working *at this point in time* on an interpretation of the destruction of Pompeii for her modern dance class final.	• Francesca is *now* working on an interpretation of the destruction of Pompeii for her modern dance class final.

(continued)

Here are some common wordy phrases that can often be replaced with just one word:

Wordy	Concise	Wordy	Concise
along the lines of	like	despite the fact that	although
subsequent to	after	at this point in time	now
by means of	by	for the reason that	because
in order to	to	in the near future	soon
have the ability to	can	in view of the fact that	because
in the event that	if	has been proved to be	is
for the purpose of	for	it would be appreciated if	please
together with	with	concerning the matter of	about
in addition to	and	prior to	before

Practice. Cut out the bloat in the following sentences by eliminating unnecessary words. Cross them out and write in any replacement words.

1. Subsequent to his special training, Sylvester had the ability to hypnotize sheep and proved to be an expert at it prior to the unfortunate incident with a ram.

2. At the gathering for the purpose of the reading of her Uncle Lester's will, Miss Primpton learned that she is the recipient of his 729 piece collection of porcelain rodents.

3. Miss Primpton was not at all pleased concerning the receipt of the porcelain rodents for the reason that what she was really hoping to inherit was the button factory.

4. Mom knows that due to the fact that teen fashion fads don't last, she will not have to put up with Stella's "gutter creature" fashion statement for long. In the near future, Stella is sure to have a new look she will hate.

5. At this point in time, Adelaide thinks her cake will win the Cakes Based on Great Literature competition in view of the fact that nobody has as of yet constructed the house in *The House of Seven Gables* out of spice cake, cinnamon sticks and Necco wafers.

6. Randolph, together with Priscilla, hopes to win first prize in the Cakes Based on Great Literature competition. In the event that the two of them win, it will be the for the reason that their triple layer presentation of Edgar Allan Poe's "The Masque of the Red Death" stunned the judges.

Name _____

Build Strong Sentences with
POWERFUL VERBS

Verbs sometimes need the help of adverbs to give readers a better idea of what is going on. But replacing the verb and the adverb with one strong verb can often relay the same meaning and have greater impact. In the following examples, notice that one verb replaces a verb and an adverb in each sentence.

Before	After
• Alexander *screamed loudly* when Scooter poked him with a toothpick during the choir's performance of Brahms' "Lullaby."	• Alexander *shrieked* when Scooter poked him with a toothpick during the choir's performance of Brahms' "Lullaby."
• Wimbleton *reacted badly* when reviewing the possible side effects of his headache medicine—side effects that included hair loss, nervous kidneys, and spontaneous combustion.	• Wimbleton *panicked* when reviewing the possible side effects of his headache medicine—side effects that included hair loss, nervous kidneys, and spontaneous combustion.
• "Yeah, right," Joey *said sarcastically*, "like I really believe that *World Book of Weird Records* dude ate a Jeep."	• "Yeah, right," Joey *sneered*, "like I really believe that *World Book of Weird Records* dude ate a Jeep."
• Archie *sings sentimentally* outside Evelyn's window every evening until she wants to throw shoes at him.	• Archie *croons* outside Evelyn's window every evening until she wants to throw shoes at him.
• Sylvester *burped loudly*.	• Sylvester *belched*.

You could say it's a "one for two" deal. One well-chosen verb can be much more effective than a weaker verb with an adverb. (You may have noticed that adverbs usually—but not always—end in "ly").

In looking for powerful verbs, a thesaurus is your best friend. Be sure to select a synonym that matches the mood of the action. For example, if you want to find a verb to replace "walk slowly," you might choose "stroll" to refer to someone window shopping. But you might choose

(continued)

"slink" to describe painfully shy Preston, walking slowly past the choir rehearsal hall so that soprano Molly Sue, on whom he has a whopping crush, doesn't see him.

If you want to find a verb to replace "talking quietly," you might choose "murmur" to describe someone whispering endearments into the ear of a loved one. You might choose "mutter" to describe a crabby child talking to himself and saying words his mother told him never to repeat.

Practice #1. Substitute one strong verb for the words in italics in each sentence below. Write the new word on the line provided.

1. The ogre *moved stealthily* up behind the troll and bopped him a good one for the tar and feather prank he'd pulled two weeks ago. _____

2. Mrs. Freytag *walked quickly* to the back of the classroom when Bobby tipped over the ant farm. _____

3. Deep inside, Hazelton *intensely disliked* inspecting asphalt for a living. _____

4. "But why can't I have another piece of pear pie?" Petunia *asked irritably*.

    _____

5. When the principal *announced loudly* over the intercom that he wanted to see Walter in his office immediately, we suspected it was Walter who painted the extra arrows on the parking lot. _____

6. "And just why," Mom *said angrily and loudly*, "are we finding it necessary to dye the dog's hair in the living room?" _____

7. Fred *hastily gathered* his things and left the scene of the bouncing UFO.

    _____

Practice #2. Write three sentences that describe how Ms. Massey reacts to situations her creative, but sometimes mischievous, kids get themselves into. Use strong verbs. She might, for example, *babble* when she notices the permanent marker "artwork" on the door of the refrigerator. How else does she react?

Name _____

Lose the Ho-Hum by Using
VIVID METAPHORS

Metaphors can add "zing" to your writing. A metaphor is a comparison of two things without using comparison words such as "like" or "as." Note the comparisons in the "after" sentences below.

Before	After
• Lee is good at math.	• Lee is a walking calculator. (*Lee's mathematical ability is being compared to a calculator.*)
• My little brother Fritzy is a handful.	• My little brother Fritzy is a monkey on wheels. (*Fritzy is being compared to an animal, already known for being active, that is moving even faster—"on wheels."*)
• The branches of the tree were noisy against my bedroom window.	• The branches of the tree were claws scraping my bedroom window. (*The noisy branches are being compared to claws.*)
• With just fifty pills, you will look great.	• With just fifty pills, you too will be an Adonis on the beach! (*You—after fifty doses of whatever substance is being advertised—will then be as good looking as that Greek god, Adonis.*)
• Talula was bitter after Osborn dumped her.	• Talula's normally sunny disposition turned to battery acid after Osborne dumped her. (*Talula's disposition is being compared to battery acid.*)

(continued)

Practice #1. Add metaphors to the sentences below to create comparisons. You may also add other details to add interest. (You may wish to change words around.) Hints are provided, though you don't have to use them.

Example

Before: Her voice sounded bad. (*Hint: Compare her voice to the noise made during some kind of accident.*)

After: Her voice was an airplane belly-landing on two miles of bad interstate.

1. The team made a loud entrance onto the football field. (*Hint: Compare the sound of the team to a group of animals or a noisy machine.*)

2. Her dress is bright. (*Hint: Compare the outfit to something bright in nature.*)

3. Stewart is having a bad day. (*Hint: Compare Stewart's day with an irritation or annoyance.*)

4. Math story problems are challenging for Winifred. (*Hint: Compare her difficulty with a disaster of some kind.*)

5. After Celia dumped him, Pedro was sad. (*Hint: Compare Pedro's heart to something damaged.*)

6. After their "Extreme Polka" class, Andy and Beverly were tired. (*Hint: Compare them to something empty or drained.*)

Practice #2. Write three more interesting sentences that include metaphors. Ideas for topics: *homework, the actions of a pet, a car accident, a beautiful sunset, loud music blaring from a car, licorice jelly beans.* (Or you may choose your own topics.)

Name _____

REVIVE
These Sentences

You have learned that you can make sentences more interesting and effective by showing instead of telling, by avoiding word overdose, by using powerful verbs, and by using vivid metaphors. Review what you have learned by using these techniques to improve the sentences below. Suggestions are provided.

Show Instead of Tell

Rewrite the following sentences to show instead of tell. Suggestions are provided.

1. It looks like Mimi likes the smell of the second brand of perfume better. (*Suggestion: Describe the expression on her face or what she said about the two brands. Naming the scents may also strengthen the sentence.*)

   _____

   _____

2. Mr. Chartreuse was not pleased with results of the test. (*Suggestion: Was it a certain facial expression that communicated this? Did he say or do something in particular that led the class to this conclusion?*)

   _____

   _____

Avoid Word Overdose

Replace the words in italics with one word. Write the replacement word on the line provided.

1. Helen soon found out that her cake tasted odd *due to the fact that* her little brother Frankie added toothpaste to the batter when she wasn't looking.

   _____

2. The magician included a refrigerator *in addition to* a llama in his disappearing act *for the reason that* it would impress the audience.

   _____

(continued)

Use Powerful Verbs

Substitute one strong action word for the words in italics. A thesaurus may help you find a stronger substitute for the verb.

1. Sammy swore he was *moving slowly and carefully* past the toothpick sculptures from the Around the World display when suddenly all 5,297 toothpicks in the Eiffel Tower replica tipped over and fell on top of the miniature Taj Mahal.

   _____

2. Sammy also *said over and over again* that he was just standing at a slight angle to get a better look at the Sand Sculptures of Historic Events when he suddenly fell right into the middle of The French Revolution.

   _____

3. For the rest of the field trip through the Winchester W. Threadbare Art Museum, Principal Wiggins *walked closely* behind Sammy to make sure there were no more "accidents" involving statues.

   _____

Use Vivid Metaphors

1. The chili dog eating contest winner's stomach is a (an) _____

   _____

   (*Suggestion: Compare his/her stomach to a large container or to something strong.*)

2. To little Timmy, the shadows on the wall were _____

   _____

   (*Suggestion: Finish the sentence with a metaphor that compares the shadows to something else–you decide what. Do you want to create a picture of something scary? Beautiful? Mysterious? Choose a comparison that will fit the image you want to create.*)

Name _____

REVIVE
These Sentences

You have learned that you can make sentences more interesting and effective by showing instead of telling, by avoiding word overdose, by using powerful verbs, and by using vivid metaphors. Review what you have learned by using these techniques to improve the sentences below.

Show Instead of tell

1. Abby had a lousy time at the fair.

2. Ned thought it was the funniest thing he had ever seen.

Avoid Word Overdose

1. In the event that part "Y" does not fit easily into part "Z," you may have inserted the zimwats incorrectly. Prior to reassembling, remove the zimwats by means of pulling on Tab X.

2. Subsequent to her retirement from the Q-Tip factory, Aunt Vesta took up bungee jumping and at this point in time is enjoying her new sport an extremely great amount.

Use Powerful Verbs

1. Bob and Joe reacted excitedly when they finally got permission to open up a Bait and Smoothie kiosk on the pier.

2. When we finally got there, Dad yelled loudly upon seeing that he had forgotten to put the lid on the paint can in the trunk of the car.

Use Vivid Metaphors

1. Chaz is sad.

2. Leonora is irritated.

Part II

Giving Sentences More Life
with Variety in

SENTENCE
PATTERNS

If you have used the activities in Part I, your students will have learned a number of ways to add interest to lifeless sentences. Now it's time to show them ways to improve their sentences through variety in sentence structure.

When sentences all have the same pattern, they have a tendency to lull readers to sleep. On the next page is a "before" and "after" example that shows how sentence variety, along with the other techniques from Part I, can add life to dull writing. You may read aloud the example, print it out to share with students, or make an overhead to share with students.

Have students compare the two versions. Look at the differences in how the sentences are constructed. What other techniques have been used to make the sentences more interesting?

Advice offered in this section:

- Lose choppiness with **compound sentences**.
- For added pep, use **prepositional phrases**.
- Add life to anemic sentences with **appositives**.
- Connect with **pairs of conjunctions**.
- Cure the blahs with **participial phrases**.
- Add oomph with **relative clauses**.
- Add interest with **subordinate clauses**.
- Add punch now and then with **short sentences**.
- Keep things nicely balanced with **parallelism**.
- Connect with **conjunctive adverbs**.
- Add interest with **infinitive phrases**.

(continued)

The Flood—Before

There was a storm. It caused flooding in our basement. The water rose three feet in two hours. The water ruined everything in our basement office. It ruined my backpack with all my schoolwork in it. It made the cat run off.

The Flood—After

During last month's storm, neither my father, who was clipping our cat Mr. Noodles' toenails at the time, nor my mother, who was alphabetizing the spices, was aware at first of the water streaming in downstairs. Since my father had cranked up the TV to catch the championship episode of *Extreme Bowling*, neither of them could hear the whoosh of the rushing water. They didn't notice it until Mr. Noodles finally escaped from Dad and hightailed it downstairs to hide in the Scratching Palace. He emitted a loud, attention-grabbing yowl as he splashed into the water. "Drat!" Dad hollered, as he realized something was drastically wrong.

When Mr. Noodles saw Dad tearing down the stairs, the cat freaked again and jumped from the top of the Scratching Palace onto Dad's head. Peeling the cat off his head, Dad sloshed his way to our brand new $1,500 computer setup. Mr. Noodles, who'd had enough of the situation, climbed through an open window. Although Dad was concerned about the cat, he was more concerned about the water already covering the computer's hard drive.

Dad, ordinarily a tough guy, began whimpering. As he took note of the other submerged office equipment, the soggy stacks of work reports, and his daughter's soaked backpack, he whimpered even more.

All was ruined.

But me? How was I handling it? The loss of my backpack? With all my books and assignments tucked inside?

Woo-hoo!

Best of all, I got a two-week extension on my five-page report on slugs of the Pacific Northwest. So, as bad as the storm was, it wasn't a total loss.

Lose Choppiness with
COMPOUND SENTENCES

There is nothing at all wrong with a short sentence, but too many short sentences in a row can create a feeling of choppiness. One solution is to sometimes combine two sentences into a compound sentence, using a *coordinating conjunction*. There are only a few coordinating conjunctions. They are:

and • but • or • for • nor • yet • so

Take a look at how the shorter sentences on the left below have been combined to make compound sentences on the right. Also notice how a comma is used before the conjunction.

Before	After
• Hillary likes Snickerdoodles. Rusty likes Oreos.	• Hillary likes Snickerdoodles, **and** Rusty likes Oreos.
• My mother enjoys alphabetizing the spices. She enjoys knitting nose warmers much more.	• My mother enjoys alphabetizing the spices, **but** she enjoys knitting nose warmers much more.
• Great Aunt Hyacinth drives her Crown Victoria to the grocery store when she has a long list. If she has to pick up just a few items, she prefers her 2007 chopped Harley Davidson with the ape hangers.	• Great Aunt Hyacinth drives her Crown Victoria to the grocery store when she has a long list, **but** if she has to pick up just a few items, she prefers her 2007 chopped Harley Davidson with the ape hangers.
• The paint department clerk asked, "Are you thinking of 'Oregon Trail Brown' for your wall? Are you leaning more toward 'Compost'?"	• The paint department clerk asked, "Are you thinking of 'Oregon Trail Brown' for your wall, **or** are you leaning more toward 'Compost'?"

(continued)

Compound Sentences *continued*

Read the paragraph below. Then notice how it changes when some of the sentences are combined to make compound sentences, as in the second paragraph.

Without compound sentences

Buzz fell head over heels for Betsy the first day of seventh grade. He really wanted to impress her. He couldn't write very well. He went to the mall and grabbed the fanciest card he could find. It had lots of flowers and sparkly things. He signed it, "Yours forever, Buzz." He gave it to her the next day. She opened it. She made a funny face. "You idiot," she hollered." This is a birthday card for a grandma!"

With compound sentences

Buzz fell head over heels for Betsy the first day of seventh grade, **and** he really wanted to impress her. He couldn't write very well, **so** he went to the mall and grabbed the fanciest card he could find. It had lots of flowers and sparkly things. He signed it, "Yours forever, Buzz," and gave it to her the next day. She opened it, **but** then she made a funny face. "You idiot," she hollered. "This is a birthday card for a grandma!"

Punctuation tip

Insert a comma before the coordinating conjunction in a compound sentence unless the two sentences you are combining are *very* short. (Example: Bob ran but Bill walked.)

Practice. The following paragraph is filled with short, choppy sentences. Rewrite it, combining some of the sentences to make compound sentences. You may need to add, delete, or rearrange words.

Geraldine was trying to remember which clown she hired for Sonny's birthday party. She wanted to hire the same one for Minnie's party. Minnie's party was on Saturday. Was it Giggles the Clown? Was it Mr. Bubblehead? Maybe it was Mr. Sniffles. Maybe it was Jiggles the Jester. It could have been Mr. Velcro. It could have been Bobo the Hobo. She couldn't remember. She decided to call the clown agency.

For Added Pep, Use

PREPOSITIONAL PHRASES

Prepositional phrases can add details to sentences and make them more interesting. A prepositional phrase is a group of words that starts with a preposition (see the list of prepositions below) and ends with a noun.

Prepositional phrases often give information that has something to do with *position*, like *where* something might be. Often, they also indicate *when* something happened. Many prepositional phrases begin with the very common preposition "of." In fact, "of" is the second most frequently used word in the English language.

Here are a few examples of sentences with prepositional phrases. The prepositional phrases are placed in parentheses.

- Just as he was walking (onto the stage), the speaker noticed the toilet paper stuck (to his shoe).
- Floyd failed his flute final when he developed a sudden case (of hiccups) (during his performance.)
- Ted's frog, Hops, escaped (on Monday) (in the biology lab).
- Hops jumped (over Professor Bodkins' collection) (of specimens) (of unusual shapes) and landed (under the crustacean display).

Some common prepositions are listed below:

aboard, about, above, across, after, against

along, among, around, at, before, behind, below, beneath

beside, between, beyond, by, concerning

despite, down, during, for, from

in, inside, into, like, near, of, off, on, onto, out

outside, over, past, regarding, since, through

throughout, till, to, toward, under, underneath, until, unto,

up, upon, with, within, without

(continued)

Prepositional Phrases *continued*

Here are some before and after examples of how prepositional phrases can make your writing more interesting. The prepositional phrases are placed in parentheses. Notice that they sometimes occur in strings, one right after the other.

Before	After
• Grandma still puts on quite a show.	• Although she's 92, Grandma still puts on quite a show (on the trampoline).
• Francis isn't quite sure what he likes best.	• Whether it is the high-pitched squeal (of the drill) or the intense odor (of the Novocain), Francis isn't quite sure what he likes best (about the dentist's office).
• Cousin Dizzy and the Polka Renegades will perform.	• Cousin Dizzy and the Polka Renegades will perform (at a fund-raiser) (for the Randolph Buntzen Middle School soccer ball fund) before hitting the road (for the Polkafest) (in Sheboygan).
• It was hard to believe what was there.	• It was hard to believe what was (underneath the pile) (of old gym socks) (in the trunk) (of his car).
• Takahiro wants to change careers.	• Takahiro wants to change careers (from Sumo wrestling) (to ice dancing).
• Gwendolyn forgot.	• (Amid the excitement) (of the Super Bowl party), Gwendolyn forgot (about the skunk) trapped (underneath the back porch.)

(continued)

Practice. Use prepositional phrases to finish the following sentences and to make them more interesting. (All prepositional phrases are in parentheses.)

1. The *Supermarket Tattler* reports that Bigfoot often appears (in the back) (of_____
   _____

2. Anna, however, was quite sure she saw Bigfoot (on top) (of_____
   _____

3. Harrison claimed he saw a flying cement truck (near_____
   _____

4. "The lawn mower's (in the living room) (by the _____
   _____)," hollered Max.

5. Stuart strapped on his gravity boots (during _____
   _____

Challenge. Write five sentences that contain prepositional phrases. Some subject ideas: *other places Bigfoot or other creatures have been spotted lately, what else Harrison claims he has seen (and where), what else is in Max's living room, or anything else that appeals to your imagination.*

1. _____
   _____

2. _____
   _____

3. _____
   _____

4. _____
   _____

5. _____
   _____

Add Life to Anemic Sentences with
APPOSITIVES

An appositive can add personality to weak, anemic sentences. So what is an appositive? It's a phrase that interrupts a sentence to give more information about one of the nouns or pronouns in the sentence. Here are some examples with the appositives in italics.

Before	After
• Mr. Macaroni has ruled our house for five years.	• Mr. Macaroni, *a black and white fur ball of attitude in the form of a hyper hamster,* has ruled our house for five years.
• Mr. Macaroni's name was inspired by an unfortunate incident.	• Mr. Macaroni's name was inspired by an unfortunate incident, *an incident involving fifty gallons of macaroni and cheese.*
• Grandpa Alfonso also plays the electric tambourine.	• Grandpa Alfonso, *winner of the senior center's Pep Band Performer of the Month contest for his rousing kazoo solos,* also plays the electric tambourine.

An appositive can help make your writing stronger, more informative, and more interesting. Take a look at the following paragraph, without appositives. Then see how it is improved *with* appositives.

Without appositives

Shirley got up late. She dressed and ate breakfast as fast as she could. She snatched her white sweater from the dryer and pulled it on. She grabbed her backpack and headed for the school bus. It wasn't until after the all-school assembly that someone told her she had a black sock stuck to the back of her sweater.

(continued)

Appositives *continued*

With appositives

Shirley, *my perfect in every way sister*, got up late the other day. She dressed and ate breakfast as fast as she could. She snatched her white sweater, *a Gucci, of course*, from the dryer and pulled it on. She grabbed her backpack and headed for school. It wasn't until after the all-school assembly, *the one where she gave her student body president campaign speech*, that someone told her she had a black sock stuck to the back of her sweater.

Practice #1. Rewrite the sentences below, inserting an appositive phrase in each. Change the wording of the sentences if you need to. Suggestions are provided. (Punctuation tip: An appositive is separated from the rest of a sentence with commas if it comes in the middle of the sentence. If it comes at the end of a sentence, it is separated from the rest of the sentence with a comma before it.)

Example

Without an appositive: The manager fired the janitor.

With an appositive: The manager fired the janitor, *the one who forgot to post the "wet paint" sign.*

1. Otis really liked the Tuesday lunch special at the Gonzo Burger Café. (*Suggestion: Add an appositive after "lunch special." What was the special?*)

2. Our dog got loose in the petting zoo. (*Suggestion: After the word "dog," add an appositive telling more about the dog.*)

3. The first time I saw Great Uncle Arbuthnot's house I understood why we hardly ever go there. (*Suggestion: After the word "house," add an appositive describing something about it.*)

4. Memory expert Elmo Doorknob claimed he just "forgot" to pay his taxes all those years. (*Suggestion: After Elmo Doorknob's name, add an appositive giving more information about him.*)

5. Buford won first prize in the school's "Unusual Talents" competition. (*Suggestion: After his name, tell what Buford did that won first prize.*)

Practice #2. Create three more sentences that include appositives. Possible subjects: *what else Otis likes about the Gonzo Burger Café, what happened when the dog got loose in the petting zoo, something else about Great Uncle Arbuthnot,* or a subject of your choice.

Name _____

Liven Up These
Hᴏ-Hᴜᴍ Sᴇɴᴛᴇɴᴄᴇs

You have learned that you can make sentences more interesting and effective by combining some short, choppy sentences into compound sentences, by using prepositional phrases to add detail, and by using appositives to add information. Review what you have learned by using one or more of these techniques to improve each sentence below. Follow the suggestion provided after each sentence.

1. Shelley came in second in the school's "Unusual Talents" competition. (*Add an apposi-tive after "Shelley" or "Unusual Talents" competition.*)

   _____

   _____

   _____

2. Hans was pretty sure the skunk was hiding. (*Add one or more prepositional phrases.*)

   _____

   _____

   _____

3. Great Aunt Azalea is coming to visit and wants to bring her pets. (*Add an appositive after "Great Aunt Azalea" or "pets."*)

   _____

   _____

   _____

4. Mitzy broke the zipper. She wasn't worried. (*Turn these two sentences into a compound sentence **and** add a prepositional phrase.*)

   _____

   _____

   _____

(continued)

5. It was cold outside. Mrs. Nantucket put a sweater on her Chihuahua. (*Turn these two sentences into a compound sentence* **and** *add an appositive after either "Mrs. Nantucket" or "Chihuahua."*)

_____

_____

_____

6. Today, Jillian added two more characters to her "favorite cartoon characters" quilt. (*Add an appositive after "Jillian" or "characters."*)

_____

_____

_____

7. Presley explained how to get to the snake zoo. (*Add one or more prepositional phrases.*)

_____

_____

_____

8. The Wriggling Family Jugglers just added two more items to their list of unusual things to juggle. (*Add an appositive after "Wriggling Family Jugglers."*)

_____

_____

_____

9. Gretel ordered a dish of Wicked Watermelon ice cream. She ordered some sprinkles to put on top. (*Turn these two sentences into a compound sentence* **and** *add at least one prepositional phrase.*)

_____

_____

_____

10. Grady had a hard time getting the stuffed frog out of the dryer vent. (*Add two or three prepositional phrases.*)

_____

_____

_____

Name _____

Liven Up These

Ho-Hum Sentences

Improve the sentences below by using the following techniques:

- Combine short, choppy sentences into **compound sentences**.
- Use **prepositional phrases** to add detail.
- Use **appositives** to add interesting information.

You don't have to use all three techniques with each sentence. Mix and match. In parentheses after each sentence you write, tell what technique or techniques you are using.

Example

Original: Buddy saw the giant dog. He hollered, "Stay! Please!"

Rewritten: When Buddy saw the giant dog, *the twelve hundred pound poodle he'd read about in the newspaper,* he hollered, "Stay! Please!"
(Added an appositive)

1. My dog Woofer wears sunglasses in the sun. When it rains he wears boots.

   _____

   _____

   _____

2. He chased the hedgehog.

   _____

   _____

   _____

3. Thelma enjoys making peach pies. She would rather track big game.

   _____

   _____

   _____

(continued)

4. Ned won the yodeling contest. Nita would have won if she hadn't inhaled a gnat.

    _____

    _____

    _____

5. Abe won second prize in the unusual vegetable contest. Claire won third prize.

    _____

    _____

    _____

6. Princess Peony finally saw Finnigan again when he rescued her.

    _____

    _____

    _____

7. Our English teacher told us that we should learn how to write compound sentences. Then she will reward us.

    _____

    _____

    _____

Bonus

Write an original sentence of your own for each of the patterns below. Subject ideas: *more about Thelma, other yodeling contest entrants, more about Princess Peony and Finnigan,* or a topic of your own.

- A compound sentence
- A sentence that includes prepositional phrases
- A compound sentence that includes prepositional phrases
- A sentence that includes an appositive
- A compound sentence that includes prepositional phrases and an appositive

Name _____

Connect with

PAIRS OF CONJUNCTIONS

Conjunctions connect words or groups of words. Some conjunctions—correlative conjunctions—are used in pairs. The name sounds a bit intimidating, but correlative conjunctions are easy to recognize and easy to use. These are all the correlative conjunctions:

both...and
not only...but also
either...or
neither...nor
whether...or

Notice how they are used in the following story.

> Ambrose has purchased one bouquet of red roses for Valentine's Day. He wants to give it to **either** Allison **or** Winifred. **Both** Allison **and** Winifred know Ambrose is a two-timer. They believe **not only** that the big red lipstick message "GET LOST, TWO-TIMER" written on the windshield of Ambrose's car **but also** the four deflated tires will tell him how they feel.

Here are some sample sentences using correlative conjunctions:

1. **Neither** my little brother **nor** my Uncle Harvey cares for Mom's chili pepper and mustard-spiced fritters.

2. Sylvester won the prize **not only** for reciting from memory the entire chapter in the tenth grade English textbook on parts of speech (including the footnotes) **but also** for staying awake while doing so.

3. **Both** collecting rubber bands of various sizes **and** constructing miniature military installations out of recyclables are my little brother's favorite pastimes.

4. "Freddy," said Mom, "I don't care **whether** you left your backpack on the Star Trek Enterprise **or** the Good Ship Lollipop, you'd better locate it by tomorrow morning—and don't give *me* that look!"

5. Clearly, it is **not only** fair **but also** necessary to honor Lester Finch of Sydney as the very first inventor of the pocket-sized UFO Neutralizer.

(continued)

Practice #1. Write an original sentence that imitates the pattern of each sentence below. In other words, keep the correlative conjunctions, but substitute your own details. Here's an example:

Original: *Both* collecting rubber bands of various sizes and colors *and* constructing miniature military installations out of recyclables are my little brother's favorite pastimes.

Rewritten: *Both* riding her bike on mountain roads *and* swimming in cold mountain lakes with her friends are two of Cecilia's favorite activities.

1. My mother plans on entering **either** her knitted Titanic replica **or** her crocheted soup can cozies in the needle crafts competition.

   _____

   _____

   _____

2. To my knowledge, **both** garlic buds **and** wormwood roots have some medicinal value, although they tend to set a kid back socially about two years.

   _____

   _____

   _____

3. **Neither** Felicia **nor** Tiffany wants to watch *Boxing for Dollars.*

   _____

   _____

   _____

Practice #2. Create two original sentences, each using a different pair of correlative conjunctions.

1. _____

   _____

   _____

2. _____

   _____

   _____

Cure the Blahs with
PARTICIPIAL PHRASES

Prepositional phrases start with prepositions, which tend to be boring little words like "of," "in," "on," etc. *Participial* phrases, on the other hand, start with something more interesting—verbs. Most of the time, these are "ing" verbs. Here are some examples of participial phrases:

- **Clutching her beloved Chihuahua Mr. Pill**, Mrs. Ballyhoo left the pet competition in a huff.

- **Believing the winning pet had an unfair advantage**, Mrs. Ballyhoo resolved to lodge a formal complaint.

- **Crawling around on a scrap of tie-dyed fabric**, the winner, a chameleon named Mellow, impressed the judges by continuously changing color.

Notice that the introductory participial phrases are followed by a comma. When a participial phrase interrupts in the middle of the sentence and is not essential to the meaning of the sentence, it is set off on both sides with a comma. When it interrupts at the end of the sentence, only one comma is needed. If the participial phrase is necessary to the meaning of the sentence, no commas at all are used. Here are some examples:

- Mr. Pill whimpered and whined, **knowing he had been humiliated by a chameleon**.

- Mellow's owner, **smiling a little smile**, counted her prize money as she walked away.

- The chameleon **scurrying around on the rainbow-colored carpet** was putting on another colorful show. (In this sentence "scurrying around on the rainbow-colored carpet" identifies which chameleon is being talked about, so it is *not* set off with commas.)

Here are some more examples of participial phrases:

- **Mastering the mysterious em-dash**, Ms. Flindersniddle's students felt they could move on to the next punctuation puzzler: the baffling ellipsis.

- **Preparing for the Pan-Pacific Punctuation Games**, Ms. Flindersniddle's students are still a little nervous about the grueling semi-colon competition.

- Ramona spotted Morley **heading for the Apostrophe Toss at the Pan-Pacific Punctuation Games**.

(continued)

Practice #1. Add a participial phrase beginning with an "ing" verb to the beginning of each of the following sentences. You may wish to add or delete words or change them around.

1. _____,

   Jed decided to back out of the swamp.

2. _____,

   Talula swore she would love Ansel—and only Ansel—forever.

Practice #2. Add a participial phrase beginning with an "ing" verb to the end of each of the following sentences.

1. The baby laughed and then started to hiccup, _____

   _____

2. Harry was pretty sure that kid was the one who spray-painted his lawn purple,

   _____

Practice #3. Add a participial phrase beginning with an "ing" verb to the middle of each of the following sentences.

1. Ms. Flindersniddle, _____

   _____, smiled when she found out the Comma Derby was the

   final competition in the Pan-Pacific Punctuation Games.

2. Quotation Mark Marathon champion Spencer Fontleroy, _____

   _____, hopes to make it to the sudden death playoffs in the

   Hyphen Match.

Practice #4. Write two original sentences with participial phrases. Suggested topic: *What else happened at the Pan-Pacific Punctuation Games?* Or choose a topic of your own.

   _____

   _____

   _____

   _____

   _____

   _____

Name _____

Add Oomph with
RELATIVE CLAUSES

Relative clauses begin with relative pronouns. There are only five relative pronouns:

who, whose, whom, which, that

Relative clauses can add interest to a sentence. They add more details about one of the nouns or pronouns in a sentence. Here are some examples of sentences before and after relative clauses have been added:

Before	After
• Jasper proudly led Oceanville's Walrus Days Parade.	• Jasper, who wore flashing red leather boots and a neon green helmet, proudly led Oceanville's Walrus Days Parade.
• Mrs. Kalamzoon announced that all those on the list can audition for roles in this year's drama club production.	• Mrs. Kalamzoon announced that all those on the list can audition for roles in this year's drama club production, **which is "Crime and Punishment, the Musical."**
• The screaming reminded Micah he had forgotten to make sure the door to the "Spiderama" was secured.	• The screaming **that came from the girls' locker room** reminded Micah he had forgotten to make sure the door to the "Spiderama" was secured.
• Ned Shoehorn is the guy who wrote *101 Uses for Dryer Lint*.	• Ned Shoehorn, **whose book *101 Uses for Soap Scum* earned him last year's "Green Housekeeping Award,"** is the guy who wrote *101 Uses for Dryer Lint*.

Punctuation tip: Use commas to separate the relative clauses from the rest of the sentence only if they introduce "extra" information not necessary to get the meaning of the sentence. If the information is necessary to the meaning of the sentence, do not use commas.

(continued)

Practice. Complete the relative clauses in the following sentences.

1. The kid with the purple hair is the one **who** _____

_____in the annual

cooking class "Snack Off" competition. *(Suggestion: What dish did he enter?)*

2. Syd, **who**_____

_____, plays the electric harp.

(Suggestion: What group does he belong to?)

3. Artist Renfro P. Sledgehammer is the award–winning sculptor of the five-ton granite

nose **that** _____

(Suggestion: Where is the sculpture displayed? Or what happened to it?)

4. The bank robber, **who** _____

_____, also used

one of the security mirrors to adjust his fake mustache. *(Suggestion: What else did he do*

that made it so easy to catch him?)

5. Besides working as a knife-thrower's assistant before she became a best-selling

author, Allison Cantaloupe was the hire-wire juggler **who** _____

_____

(Suggestion: What did she juggle up there?)

Challenge. Write three sentences of your own that include relative clauses. Topic ideas:
*unusual electric instruments, what caused that smell in the fridge, Refro P. Sledgehammer's other
odd sculptures,* or topics of your choice.

1. _____

_____

_____

2. _____

_____

3. _____

_____

Bring These Incomplete Sentences
To Life

Practice. You have learned that you can make sentences more interesting and effective by using pairs of conjunctions (or correlative conjunctions), participial phrases, and relative clauses. Review what you have learned by using these techniques to complete the sentences below.

Pairs of Conjunctions

1. Cal decided to both_____

    and _____ in the *Earth's*

    Got Talent competition.

2. Henrietta was surprised to find not only _____ but

    also _____ when she opened the refrigerator door.

Participial Phrases

1. _____, Jose saw a porcupine scurrying

    around the backyard and popping all the birthday balloons.

2. Mr. Bobblehead tried to look innocent, _____

    _____

3. _____, D.J. ran as fast as he could from

    the exploding marshmallow factory.

Relative Clauses

1. The winner of this year's hot tamale eating contest is Hector Waterfaucet, _____

    _____

2. Renee finally found the source of the smell, _____

    _____

Challenge. Write one sentence that includes a pair of correlative conjunctions, a participial phrase, and a relative clause. Topic: the *Earth's Got Talent* competition or a subject of your choice.

Name _____

Bring These Incomplete Sentences
To Life

You have learned that you can make sentences more interesting and effective by using pairs of conjunctions (or correlative conjunctions), participial phrases, and relative clauses. Review what you have learned by following the suggestions after each item below.

Pairs of Conjunctions

1. Chloe, known for her offbeat sense of style, wasn't sure what to wear to the safari-themed dance. (*Add another sentence describing Chloe's wardrobe choices. Use the correlative conjunctions "either" and "or" in the sentence.*)

   _____

   _____

   _____

2. Little Will was going through a phase where he would only eat yellow-colored food. (*Add another sentence that describes two yellow foods Little Will will eat. Use the correlative conjunctions "both," and "and" in the sentence.*)

   _____

   _____

   _____

3. Carlton has unusual pets. (*Add another sentence about two of Carlton's pets. Use the correlative conjunctions "not only," and "but also."*)

   _____

   _____

   _____

Participial Phrases

1. Heloise saw the hairy bug her brother told her about. (*Add another sentence about Heloise's discovery, using a participial phrase that begins with the verb "screaming."*)

   _____

   _____

   _____ *(continued)*

2. From lighting cheeseburger-scented candles to munching purple popcorn, Nelly has found several unusual ways to help her study for tests. (*Add another sentence about how Nelly studies, using a participial phrase that begins with the verb "wearing."*)

_____

_____

_____

3. The last time Brewster was in a fancy gift shop he tipped over a display of glass toads. (*Add another sentence about Brewster's visit to the gift shop, using a participial phrase that begins with the verb "stumbling."*)

_____

_____

_____

Relative Clauses

1. Concert pianist Niles Flamingo can play the piano very fast. He recently performed the "Minute Waltz" in 50 seconds. (*Create a sentence that combines both of the sentences above and also uses a relative clause starting with "who." Change or delete words as necessary.*)

_____

_____

_____

2. The stuff in a container in the bottom of the refrigerator was moving. It turned out to be the long-forgotten fish and eggplant casserole. (*Create a sentence that combines both of the sentences above and also uses a relative clause starting with "that." Change or delete words as necessary.*)

_____

_____

_____

3. Francine got her hair dyed the day before the wedding by a new stylist. (*Add a relative clause to the sentence above to make it more interesting. Change or delete words as necessary.*)

_____

_____

_____

Name _____

Add Interest with
SUBORDINATE CLAUSES

A subordinate clause is a part of a sentence that cannot stand alone, even though it has a subject and a predicate. It is introduced by a subordinate conjunction. Here is a list of common subordinate conjunctions used to introduce subordinate clauses:

**after, although, as, as if, as long as, as though
because, before, if, in order that, provided that, since
so that, that, though, unless, until, when, where, whereas, while**

The sentences below show the subordinate clause in italics:

D.J. had just spent three hours painting a fence bright red
when something told him to check to make sure he was at the correct address.

After D.J. finished painting over the bright red with three coats of white (no charge, of course),
he started work on the fence he was supposed to paint.

Punctuation tip: When a subordinate clause begins a sentence, it is usually followed by a comma. A comma is not usually used when the clause is at the end of a sentence.

More sample sentences using subordinating conjunctions:

- **Since my father had cranked up the TV to catch an episode of *Extreme Bowling,*** the sound drowned out the whoosh of storm water flooding into the basement.

- **Although my father is pretty addicted to *Extreme Bowling,*** I'm sure he would give it up in a heartbeat if *Offtrack Beetle Racing* came on at the same time.

- Many people pepper their papers with commas **since they are uncertain about where to insert them.**

- Ed had to sell the worm farm **because his roller derby investments took a dive.**

- **Since Mom began drinking the new energy pop KaBoom,** her knitting output has steadily increased.

(continued)

Practice. Add subordinate clauses to the following sentences. Use a different subordinate conjunction in each sentence.

Example

No subordinate clause: Come here and help me wash the windows.

With subordinate clause added: *If* you're not too busy keeping the couch warm, come here and help me wash the windows.

1. Our cat Mr. Noodles hates to have his toenails clipped.

   _____

   _____

   _____

2. Boomer's favorite paint names to date include "Rusted Tin," "Dirt," and "WD-40."

   _____

   _____

   _____

3. Zippy the Amazing Beetle is Dad's favorite racing beetle.

   _____

   _____

   _____

4. Horton suggested filling the swamp with tapioca pudding.

   _____

   _____

   _____

5. Amelia is a longtime fan of the metal band Hammer & Nails.

   _____

   _____

   _____

Sentence CPR • Copyright © 2010 by Phyllis Beveridge Nissila • Cottonwood Press, Inc. • www.cottonwoodpress.com
52

Add Punch Now and Then with
SHORT SENTENCES

Sometimes, the fewer the words the better. A short sentence or a sentence fragment thrown in among longer ones can add variety and punch to your work.

Yes, sentence fragments are acceptable once in a while if you choose to use one for effect *intentionally.* That's not the same as using one by accident.

Examples:

- Jiggy's band Wilted Lettuce will perform Tuesday night at seven o'clock in the barn. *Bring beans.*

- Act now and we will send you the faux fur traveling coat with the mock leather insets and imitation silver buckles in your color choice of oatmeal or pumice for just five easy payments! *But, wait!* Call in the next seven minutes and get a free hanger!

- Taxidermist Finias P. Underwear never saw roadkill he couldn't stuff. *Until today.*

- "So," began Professor Anklebone, "what is your perception of the existential dichotomy of the parallel indicators of pi?"

  "Dude?" replied Scooter.

- He knew as soon as the car rounded the corner and they spotted the Quenton Peabody Memorial String Museum that they were driving around in circles. *Again.*

- Dear Mom, life is good here at Camp Wa-Hoo-Ee. Although the floodwaters washed away almost all of the food, the supply of Twinkies and beef jerky is okay. Although all the mattresses on the lower bunks got soaked, the water also drowned all the bugs, and nobody's seen the bear for two days. *Send itch cream.* Love, Wally.

- Hargraves is beginning to feel uneasy about the child of the family who moved in next door. First there were the two-dozen spike-toothed pumpkin zombies on the front porch on Halloween. Then there were "The Snowmen of the Apocalypse" lining the front driveway. *What's next?*

(continued)

Practice. For each paragraph below, add a short sentence before, between, or after existing sentences. Draw an arrow to the place where you want the sentence to go.

1. Although electric zithers are gaining popularity among indy punkers, they were first used by the garage band Painted Toenails in 1968. The Toenails' lead guitarist "Ty Dye" (Quenton Smythers, originally from Eugene, Oregon, now an insurance salesman in Toledo) is modest about his influence, however.

   _____

2. Excited about winning first place at this year's Yarn Spinners' Knit-off, my mother has decided to knit Noah's Ark, animals included, for next year's competition. She is in the process of selecting which animal pairs to include. Besides the usuals, she thinks the addition of alpacas, otters, and wombats ought to impress the judges.

   _____

3. The International Thumb Wrestling Federation is having its next championship meet in Drain, Oregon. Thumb wrestling enthusiasts from all over the world are expected to attend this three day event. Drain beat Boring, Oregon, in a fierce battle to host the event.

   _____

4. We just found out that cousins Otis and Bo are coming for the holidays again, and Mom is not happy. After they left last year she found gobs of used gum stuck underneath the kitchen chairs. The boys didn't bathe for a week, they ate like pigs, and they had armpit burping contests. Mom's thinking of moving and not leaving a forwarding address.

   _____

5. Glick, Lord Hemisphere's sidekick/slave was feeling especially unappreciated. It was hard being at His Lordship's beck and call all the time. It was annoying to hear, "Glick, do this," and, "Glick, do that," day in and day out. In short, Glick was fed up with slavery. Was it too much to ask, he wondered, for a weekend off now and then to relax at the Boar's Head Inn or hunt dragons?

   _____

Keep Things Nicely Balanced with

PARALLELISM

When two or more ideas are constructed in a similar way, or in a similar grammatical form, they are considered *parallel*. The most common form of parallelism involves a list or series. A sentence flows better and is easier to understand if the items in the series or list are in the same form. Examples:

- Andrea, who normally goes for colors like *atomic tangerine*, *neon eggplant*, and *blood red*, decided to dye her hair brown.
    (Each item listed is a color, with a descriptive word before it.)

- As far as Liza can tell, the only exercise Jud gets is *couch pressing*, *channel surfing*, and *pretzel crunching*.
    (Each item listed is a form of exercise—at least according to Jud—using an "ing" verb.)

Other forms of parallelism are phrases and clauses that are constructed in the same way. Three examples:

- Mother declared, "You'd better have a really good explanation this time for *knocking* over the rubber tree, *flipping* the piano, and *putting* all those holes in the ceiling."
    (The parallel parts start with an "ing" verb.)

- "*Not* now, *not* later, *not* ever!" hollered Astrid, when Giorgio asked her to marry him for the seventy-third time.
    (The parallel parts start with "not".)

- After hearing what was for lunch in the cafeteria, little Winthrop explained that he quite preferred *pasta primavera to macaroni and cheese* and *raspberry smoothies to milk*.
    (The parallel parts list what picky little Winthrop prefers to what is on the menu.)

(continued)

Practice #1. Create parallelism in the following sentences using the suggestions.

1. Beginning power tool jugglers are prone to _____

   _____

   _____ *(Start with "ing" verbs.)*

2. WARNING: Before assembling your very own nuclear submarine, be sure to _____

   _____

   _____ *(Start with verbs.)*

3. Benson found another ointment to try on his rash but decided against that one, too,

   when he read about its possible side effects: _____

   _____

   _____ *(Start with "ing" verbs.)*

Practice #2. Change the following sentences so that the parts in each are parallel.

1. Our hamster Twitch is so obsessed with his hamster ball he would roll around the house
   all morning, all afternoon, and during the night if we let him. _____

   _____

   _____

   _____

2. According to the latest issue of the *Supermarket Tattler*, the Ammonia People from
   Neptune are the ones hiding Elvis, making banjo patterns in corn fields, and they are
   also trying to get in touch with Big Foot.

   _____

   _____

   _____

3. Leroy's favorite Golden Boot Award country bands are the 2002 winner Outta Luck,
   Bad Habits in 2004, and that other band named The Abner Hooligan Jug Band that
   won in 2008.

   _____

   _____

   _____

(continued)

4. Legend has it that Igor of the ancient Fo-fum Clan whomped the ogre, then he beaned the troll and kicked the gnome.

   _____

   _____

   _____

5. Benson was considering trying the ointment for his rash until he learned that possible side effects include spontaneous boils, and irritable liver, and that your gall bladder could suddenly explode.

   _____

   _____

   _____

6. "To get to the castle," began the gnome, "you must slog through the stinking swamp; second, ascend the steps that are very slimy; and then thrash through the thistly thicket."

   _____

   _____

   _____

Name _____

Inject Some Energy into
THESE SENTENCES

You have learned that you can make sentences more interesting and effective by using subordinate clauses, by using short sentences now and then, and by using parallelism. Review what you have learned by using these techniques to finish the sentences below.

Finish the Subordinate Clauses

Add a subordinate clause to each sentence below. The subordinate conjunction is provided for you.

1. Demi agreed to take her little brother and his friends to see *Night of the Rattlesnakes, 3-D*, **if** _____

   _____

   _____

2. "Listen, Cyd," whispered Leon, "I think the giant chicken saw us. Be careful **when** _____

   _____

   _____

3. **Although** she _____

   _____,

   Grandma agreed to ride the "Rollercoaster Scream Express" with Ryan, just this once.

4. Smedley preferred expensive cologne, Italian shoes, Mister Swell suits, and caviar, **whereas** Slick _____

   _____

   _____

5. **Since** _____,

   Mindy has been sighing a thousand sighs, crying a thousand tears, and throwing darts at Jack's picture.

   (continued)

Short Sentences. Add at least one short sentence to the long sentences in each selection below. Draw an arrow to the place where the sentence should be inserted.

Jeb's Tips on How to Succeed in School, Part 1

• Come prepared for class with all the books and other tools necessary to do your best. Arrange everything neatly in front of you so that you are prepared to perform any task required. Power down all cell phones, iPods, iPhones, MP3 players, beepers, buzzers, flashers, blinkers, and any other gadgets that might distract you and everyone else and cause your teacher to give you even more looks you don't want.

    (Suggestion: Is there any "look" in particular someone might want to avoid?)

_____

• Show respect to all school staff including teachers, guidance counselors, secretaries, attendance clerks, maintenance technicians, and crossing guards. Do not address them with terms like "Yo," "Teach," or "Dude." Instead call them by their names preceded by a title, like "Mr. Sparkplug," "Principal Vanderhoovennoggin," or "Sister Angelica").

    (Suggestion: What else you should avoid doing? Add a short sentence that starts with "Don't" or "Especially don't.")

_____

Parallelism. Complete the following sentences, making all additions parallel in form.

1. The three main ingredients in Cousin Curly's five-alarm chili are _____
_____, and _____

2. We're pretty sure the iguana is hiding _____,
_____, or _____

Create a sentences of your own, according to the instructions below.

3. Using parallelism, create a sentence that includes three directions about what to do before assembling your new piano. Begin each of the three directions with a verb.

_____

_____

4. Using parallelism, create a sentence about three uses for Aunt Germaine's All-Purpose Cream.

_____

_____

Name _____

Inject Some Energy into

THESE SENTENCES

Subordinate Clauses. Finish the sentences below using a subordinate clause. Start the clause with the subordinate conjunction in bold.

1. Mark insisted on wearing his Superman costume to school **because** _____

   _____

2. Ray's favorite meal was salad, meatloaf, mashed potatoes, and apple pie, **whereas** Poncho liked_____

3. "Okay, you can go to the flea market," said Mom, "**as long as** _____

   _____

Short Sentences. Place one short sentence or sentence fragment somewhere in the selection below. Draw an arrow showing where the sentence belongs.

First, Bridget tied the little pink bib with the rosebud print around Susie's neck. Next, she gently pulled on two pairs of little white ruffled socks and then carefully fitted a lace bonnet on Suzie's head. But just as Bridget started to put the matching lace shawl around Suzie's shoulders, the bulldog woke up, sniffed at her strange outfit, and ran straight for a mud puddle.

_____

Parallelism. Finish these sentences with parallel lists, phrases, or clauses.

1. Sasha's collections of _____, _____, and _____ won her first prize in the Unusual Collections Competition.

2. Raul watched as the man in the mattress suit advertising a sale at Mattress City _____, _____, and_____ on the street corner.

Name _____

Connect with
CONJUNCTIVE ADVERBS

Conjunctive adverbs—the name sounds a bit like a disease. But conjunctive adverbs really have the same useful function as tendons and ligaments; they connect things. Here are a list of common conjunctive adverbs:

accordingly • also • anyway • besides • certainly

consequently • conversely • finally • furthermore • hence

however • incidentally • indeed • instead • likewise

meanwhile • moreover • nevertheless • next • nonetheless

otherwise • similarly • specifically • still • subsequently

then • therefore • thus

When a conjunctive adverb is connecting two independent clauses, it needs some help. A comma isn't considered "strong" enough to use between the two clauses. Instead a semicolon is used, with a comma going after the conjunctive adverb. This sounds more complicated than it is. Take a look at the following examples:

- Aunt Lysteria cooks a lot**; however,** she has yet to master any dish with more than three ingredients.
- I haven't seen Myrna since the last Drum and Bugle Corps road trip**; nevertheless,** I'd recognize that high-pitched whine anywhere.
- Maggie is the producer of the hit musical, *101 Accordions***; incidentally,** she also plays the part of Ursula, the bagpipe tuner.

Another way to handle the punctuation is to turn the two clauses into two separate sentences, using a period instead of a semicolon between them. Here are two examples:

- My little brother apologized profusely. **Nonetheless,** Mom took away his BB gun and he had to pay Mr. Sweeney for all 73 tomato plants.
- Jeb and Hortense sat blissfully sipping chamomile tea. **Meanwhile,** the mildew in the downstairs shower silently spread to three more tiles.

(continued)

Practice #1. Punctuate the following sentences correctly.

1. "I'm particularly receptive to compliments today," said Lilly still Chip went on with the engine overhaul.
2. Aurillia decided against joining Future Game Show Hosts of America instead she took up the tuba.
3. In the crime scene investigative drama *CSI North Dakota*, bad guy Lenny the Lip was replaced by Joey Carburetor nevertheless ratings stalled.

Practice #2: Use conjunctive adverbs to connect the following sets of independent clauses. Rewrite the sentences, punctuating and capitalizing correctly. Change or rearrange words if needed.

1. Uncle Harvey loves to make "Black and Blue Casserole," which features black cumin and blue fenugreek. That dish makes my little brother throw up.

_____

_____

_____

2. Spices starting with the letter "C" make my brother William sneeze. He also dislikes Mom's chive and chili chimichangas.

_____

_____

_____

3. The dishes my little brother does like are usually seasoned with "L" spices like licorice, lime, and lemon. He has never met an "O" spice he doesn't like.

_____

_____

_____

Practice #3. Write three sentences of your own using semicolons and conjunctive adverbs. Subject ideas: *more about Uncle Harvey's cooking,* or a topic of your choice.

Add Interest with
INFINITIVE PHRASES

Another way to add interest and detail to sentences is to add infinitive phrases. Infinitive phrases can be added to the beginning of a sentence, the middle, or the end, but here we will use them just to start sentences.

An infinitive phrase is a group of words that starts with the word "to" and includes a simple verb or action word. Examples: *to find, to impress, to get.* The phrase may also include other words.

Examples

- *To find his way through the Bog of Fear*, Prince Wilhelm used his OnStar car safety device.
- *To get to the hospital faster*, Bruno's girlfriend took Fancher Road to Highway 20.
- *To see if Elvis was really selling ATVs at Big Al's Motor Mania*, Tom hopped on his bike and headed for Big Al's.
- *To make sure the sculptor had everything he needed*, the art studio supply clerk ordered two tons of marble, a ton of cement, twelve chisels of various kinds, seven hammers of various sizes, and 350 glass eyeballs.

Punctuation tip: Put a comma after an infinitive phrase at the beginning of a sentence, as in the examples above.

Practice #1. Complete the following sentences.

1. To find _____, the dog's owner installed a video camera in the kitchen.

2. To see _____, Mallory and Chuck looked out the back window.

3. To get _____, Boris and Elrod took Galactic Express # 9.

4. To understand _____, Betty got out her electronic translator.

(continued)

Practice #2. Complete the infinitive phrases.

1. To figure out _____, Lemuel turned to page 127 of the instruction manual for his new Whizmadoodle.

2. To get to _____, the explorer had to ride a goat.

3. To help _____, the sheep herders organized a tamale feed.

4. To make _____, Edna needed six more sacks of flour, two more sacks of sugar, five dozen eggs, a quart of blue food coloring, and a really big pan.

5. To win _____, Barney was prepared to climb the highest mountains, swim the most treacherous rivers, ride the roughest roads, lift the heaviest weights, and even single-handedly chaperone a bus load of six-year-olds to and from a field trip to the candy factory.

Practice #3. Complete the following sentences, using an infinitive phrase to begin each. In each case, the individual involved is trying to solve some kind of problem.

1. To _____, the new animal

   trainer _____

2. To _____, the lost tour guide

   _____

3. To _____, the irritated

   librarian _____

4. To _____,

   the nervous public speaker _____

Practice #4. Write an original sentence with an infinitive phrase. Suggested topics: *more about Lemuel's Wizmadoodle or Edna's baking,* or a topic of your choice.

_____

_____

_____

Name _____

Time to
PRACTICE

You have learned that you can make sentences more interesting by using conjunctive adverbs and infinitive phrases. Review what you have learned by using these techniques to finish the sentences below.

Conjunctive Adverbs. Use an appropriate conjunctive adverb to combine the sentences in each item below.

1. Jill has so far saved only $14.98 toward the $50,000 she needs to open a potato chip factory. She will pursue her dream.

   _____

   _____

2. Having just found out she is allergic to lions, Loretta turned down the job offer with the circus. She accepted a position teaching middle school English.

   _____

   _____

3. After years of musical training on several instruments, Greg decided to join a rock and roll band. There didn't seem to be much call for flugelhorn players, bassoonists, or harpists.

   _____

   _____

Infinitive Phrases. Start each sentence below with an infinitive phrase.

1. To _____,
   Mr. Jones dressed up like a math story problem teacher last Halloween.

2. To _____,
   the camp counselor assured the little campers that there were no gorillas waiting for them behind the outhouse.

Challenge. Write a sentence that uses at least one conjunctive adverb *and* one infinitive phrase. Possible topics: *more about Loretta's experience teaching middle school English, details about Greg's rock and roll band,* or a topic of your choice.

Name _____

Time to

PRACTICE

You have learned that you can make sentences more interesting by using conjunctive adverbs and infinitive phrases. Review what you have learned by using these techniques to finish the sentences below.

Conjunctive Adverbs. Use an appropriate conjunctive adverb to combine the sentences in each item below.

1. Just as little Libby came to understand the gurgle-uck-duk-duk-duk-duk sound at night was the refrigerator itself and not a monster within, she became aware of other sounds that made her lie awake in the dark for hours. Her mother had to send her to a sleep therapist.

    _____

    _____

2. Reactions to the boil ointment may include vertigo, clown hallucinations, and swollen knee caps. It is not a good idea to use it if you develop these symptoms.

    _____

    _____

Infinitive phrases. Start each sentence below with an infinitive phrase.

1. To _____,
    Carleton added a dash of pepper, a pinch of salt, and a can of sardines.

2. To _____,
    make sure your garage _____

Challenge

Write a sentence that uses **both** a conjunctive adverb **and** an infinitive phrase. Suggested topics: *More about little Libby's problems, side effects of a medication, what else Carleton did while cooking,* or a topic of your choice.

Name _____

Practice Adding Life to
MORE YAWNERS

The "Yawners" below need help. Rewrite them, adding life and interest. Use at least three of the following tips somewhere in your rewrites:

Use details • Use active voice • Use fresh similes • Show instead of tell
Avoid word overdose • Use powerful verbs • Use vivid metaphors

Also use at least five of the following kinds of sentence patterns somewhere in your rewrites:

compound sentence • sentence with prepositional phrase • sentence with appositive
sentence with correlative conjunctions • sentence with participial phrase
sentence with relative clause • sentence with subordinate clause • short sentence
sentence with parallel constructions • sentence with conjunctive adverb
sentence with infinitive phrase

Yawner #1. The band got stuck in traffic. The traffic report said the gridlock could last a long time. A semi-truck-load of fruit had tipped over. The band members were already late for rehearsal. They decided to rehearse right there. The news reported on it later.

Yawner #2. It was Zippy the beetle's first race. In the first lap, his opponent raced past him but then got stuck on something on the racing track. Zippy raced ahead and won the race.

Yawner #3. My mom entered a knitting competition. She thought her project, "Noah's Ark," would win. Mrs. Renoir's knitting project was good, too. Mom decided to add a few more pieces to her project.

Yawner #4. My little brother likes to glue things together. He glued together a lot of stuff to make a miniature space lab. He's gluing things together right now to make a fort while Mom is busy cleaning up the basement after the storm. He's using some of her pots and pans.

Yawner #5. Little Libby got a new doll. It was the kind that talks. Her parents got it at the factory seconds outlet. They soon found out why it was a "second." It didn't sound or talk like a doll. It sounded and talked like an action figure.

Practice Adding Life to
MORE YAWNERS

The "Yawners" below need help. Rewrite them, adding life and interest. Use at least three of the following tips somewhere in your rewrites:

Use details • Use active voice • Use fresh similes • Show instead of tell

Avoid word overdose• Use powerful verbs • Use vivid metaphors

Also use at least five of the following kinds of sentence patterns somewhere in your rewrites:

compound sentence • sentence with prepositional phrase • sentence with appositive

sentence with correlative conjunctions • sentence with participial phrase

sentence with relative clause • sentence with subordinate clause • short sentence

sentence with parallel constructions • sentence with conjunctive adverb

sentence with infinitive phrase

Yawner #1
Dear Jim,
I've lost my pet! Have you seen him? He's a little unusual looking. He does tricks. He's a picky eater. He will come to you if you yodel a tune he likes.
B.J.

Yawner #2
To: Discount Realtors
From: The Smiths
Re: The house for sale on 8th Avenue
We're afraid the house we looked at on 8th Avenue isn't quite what we want. There are a number of reasons for this.

Yawner #3
It was easy to see why they won the "most original band" award in the Battle of the Bands contest. They played unusual instruments. They played many styles of music. Their outfits were really different. They had interesting special effects.

For the Teacher:
MORE IDEAS FOR REVIEW

The following games, competitions, and activities suggestions are designed to help students remember and use the writing tips (Part I) and sentence patterns (Part II) presented in this book.

Writing Tips at a Glance	Sentence Patterns at a Glance
Use details.	compound sentence
Use active voice.	sentence with **prepositional phrases**
Use fresh similes.	sentence with **appositives**
Show instead of tell.	sentence with **correlative conjunctions**
Avoid word overdose.	sentence with **participial phrases**
Use powerful verbs.	sentence with **relative clauses**
Use vivid metaphors.	sentence with **subordinate clauses**
	short sentence
	sentence with **parallel constructions**
	sentence with **conjunctive adverbs**
	sentence with **infinitive phrases**

1. Photocopy the lists above, cut the items apart, and put them into two containers—one for writing tips and one for sentence patterns. Try some or all of these ideas for review and practice:

   - Use a few minutes at the beginning or end of class for sentence writing. Have a student draw an item from one of the containers, and then have everyone write a sentence using that writing tip or sentence pattern.

- Have a student or several students in turn draw from the containers. Ask students to use the items drawn to complete a group or individual writing project or homework assignment.
- Have student teams compete within a time limit to see who can create a sentence representing whatever writing tip or sentence patter is drawn. For even more fun, have the students draw odd or funny sentence subjects as well. (Students themselves might come up with subjects for a subject container.) For an extra challenge, have students draw both a writing tip *and* a sentence pattern.

2. Have students work in groups to create interesting sentences that follow each sentence pattern. Collect the sentences, review for appropriateness, cut them apart, and put them in a container. Divide the class into teams and have each team, in turn, try to identify what writing tips and/or sentence patterns they see as the items are drawn.

3. Use writing tips and/or sentence patterns in round robin story writing:
   - Each student picks a writing tip or sentence pattern from a container. Depending on the size of the class, two or more students may draw the same one.
   - Brainstorm story starters, or offer a list for students to choose from.
   - Each student begins a story using his/her writing tip or sentence pattern in one of the opening sentences.
   - When the time is up (a few minutes), students pass their stories to the person on their right.
   - Each student adds to the story passed to him or her. At least one of the sentences added must include the writing tip or sentence pattern drawn earlier.
   - The rotation continues (allowing more time for each story segment as the stories get longer) until the time is up. Remind the students to use their writing tip or sentence pattern each time they add to a story.
   - In the last go-around, students need to end their stories. (Using "And then I woke up" is not allowed.) They also need to title the story.

Note: It's a good idea to suggest that students use their writing tips or sentence patterns right away because it's easy to lose track of time. You might also want to have them underline the sentence representing their tip or pattern. For review later, you could read aloud an underlined sentence and ask the class to identify which writing tip or sentence pattern it represents.

4. Assign a "yawner" from "More Yawners" (pages 67-68) for individual students or teams to expand using assigned writing tips and/or sentence patterns. Allow plenty of time for this activity. Students may change facts or details as needed and incorporate extra sentences if needed.

Answer Keys

Sample
ANSWERS

Bring Sentences to Life with Details
Page 10, Practice #1

1. Sal and Ahmed finally saw the "Singing Earthworm" on YouTube.
2. Never one to turn down a dare, Boris actually drank the cottage cheese and molasses smoothie.
3. "Baba mookie?" asked little Baby Nick, to which Mom, who somehow knew exactly what he meant, replied, "Maybe later."
4. All three friends agreed that *Revenge of the Mutant Poodles* was a creepy movie.
5. Michelle and Lana exploded with giggles at the sight of the rooster in a tutu.
6. Jake panicked and got the hiccups just as he began his first ever harmonica solo.
7. Fionna glared at Forrest when he presented her with a table saw for their first anniversary.
8. Polly and Mimi fled back to their car when they discovered that #14 Elm Street was not the location of the bridal shower, but a reptile museum.
9. My brother and I were so hungry we scarfed down several big chunks of the giant combination pizza someone had left in the lunchroom before we noticed that the pepperoni was covered with green fuzz.
10. Maxine, my goldfish, plopped right into the middle of my alphabet soup when Karl accidentally tipped over the fishbowl.

Page 10, Practice #2

1. "Youch!" Mr. Fitzgibbons hollered when the cat went for his toupee.
2. "Dude," declared Sky.
3. "Yo," replied Jon.
4. "Here's what I want," noted A.J.: "Five regular hot dogs, no onions, just a little catsup, and mustard on the side; four chili dogs with just a little cheese on the side and one on a wheat bun; three cheeseburgers, no pickles or onions on two of them and a little relish on the side; two large fries with a little ranch dipping sauce on the side unless you have honey mustard; and a banana."
5. "Anything with that banana?" the concession worker responded, with a little sarcasm on the side.

Light a Fire Under Tired Sentences by Using Active Voice
Page 12, Practice #1

1. Crenshaw hopes that Cloris doesn't notice the fungus.
2. Mortimer P. Windjammer High School hosted the stilt-dancing competition for the third year in a row.
3. Aunt Balista made the kelp and radish soufflé.
4. Very soon after dinner Mom regretted that she made us eat Aunt Balista's soufflé.
5. Pietro quickly found the pan of red paint the puppies had been playing in.

Page 12, Practice #2

1. Timmy expected another sleepless night after watching *Night of the Melting Eyeballs.*
2. Grandma has taken up wild boar hunting now that Grandpa is in the nursing home.
3. Dr. Feldon Bazooka has just announced a career switch from psychiatry to cage wrestling.

4. Because she will be needing extra money, Aunt Gladdy is planning to teach the "Chicken Dance" on YouTube.

5. "Why didn't you tell me that this parrot blurts out, 'Whoa! Who stinks?' at random intervals?" Mrs. Winthrop Overstreet asked the pet store owner.

Page 12, Practice #3

1. Frederick, the armor designer, noted a snag in Lord Hemisphere's chainmail.

2. Damian wrote love letters to Twyla Tennessee, Hannah Montana's alleged cousin twice removed.

Draw Attention to What you Say with Fresh Similes
Page 14, Practice #1

1. Gwyneth popped her bubble gum for the twenty-seventh time that evening, which is another reason Alfred began avoiding her like a long list of chores.

2. Although he felt like an ox in a hockey rink, Bubba promised Wendy he would take the ballet workshop with her.

3. Keisha changed the oil in the cement truck for her boyfriend, who thought she was as sweet as a new paint job on a '65 Camaro to do that.

4. When she saw what her three-year-old had done with old shoe polish he found in a box in the cupboard, Eva cried like a ballerina with a broken toe on the night of her debut.

5. "I will *not* sit near you!" Tricia said to Buddy. "You're eating like a two-year-old who is learning to use a spoon!"

6. Little Timmy looked as pale as a boiled egg after viewing the Weird Science Network special on those little bugs that can crawl right through your ear drum and lay their eggs in your brain while you sleep.

Page 14, Practice #2

1. Bubba was as nervous as a contestant on *High Wire Amateur Hour* when he attempted his first pirouette in the ballet class.

2. Little Timmy was shaking like a puddle in an earthquake after viewing another Weird Science Network special: *Dust Mites and Other Microscopic Monsters Living on Your Skin.*

Breathe Life into These Yawners, Review #1
Page 15, Practice #1

1. It was a peaceful vacation except for the nightly yodeling competitions in campsite number six.

2. After Murphy ate the tuna casserole, he was as sick as a pit bull that swallowed a chunk of 10-day-old dead squirrel.

3. The batter hit the baseball out of the ball field and across the highway where it landed, finally, in someone's freshly laid cement.

4. In my opinion, the Tilt-a-Hurl was the dizziest, most exciting ride at the carnival.

5. What sounded like a very faint "Help me!" coming from the shelves of specimen bottles in the back of the biology lab surprised Dr. Wilson when she was working late one night.

Page 15, Practice #2

Surprisingly, Maria was as cool as glass when Anderson announced he was calling off their engagement. Later, when it hit her, she was as mad as a swarm of hornets chasing an exterminator. Her mother had already ordered dozens of yellow roses, a seven-tiered wedding cake, and 400 invitations. She had booked the Mariachi Amigos months ago for the reception. After thinking it over, Maria decided to have a party anyway. The only thing missing would be Anderson.

Breathe Life into These Yawners, Review #2
Page 16, Practice

1. The first time Kim tried to make music on her new clarinet, she thought it sounded more like a broken foghorn than a musical instrument. She persisted, even though her brothers and sisters started keeping their bedroom doors closed and wearing earplugs. Eventually her playing sounded more like a foghorn that was *not* broken. "That's progress," said Kim optimistically.

2. Unfortunately, by the time Contestant #42 noticed the ants, the judges were already dipping into bowls of her Twenty Bean Soup. They ate heartily and commented on the interesting crunch to the soup, "so subtle and intriguing." Contestant #42 kept smiling and kept her mouth shut.

3. All these years later, Ralph still cringes remembering his first day of middle school when, in a big hurry, he discovered the third door on the right was not the boys' bathroom. His face looked like an overripe tomato as he plunged back into the hallway, followed by the sound of seven girls screaming. Unfortunately, six eighth grade boys noticed his mistake and made sure he remembered it for a very long time.

4. "For the last time," hollered the driver, "I don't care if that mangy varmint *is* as harmless as a doodle bug; he's not riding *my* bus!" Little Angela refused to budge. She clutched the puppy inside her jacket and just stared up at the driver with her big brown eyes, knowing that, eventually, he would have to back down.

Perk Up Sentences by Showing Instead of Telling
Page 18, Practice

1. Matilda learned to tie herself in a knot and wound up a finalist on *America's Got Talent!*
2. "Insurance salesman, my eye," said Dad, watching the strange little man walk away. "If you ask me, I'd say he's just off the mother ship!"
3. Ziggy made Mr. Lee's hair turn completely white during the first on-road Driver's Education lesson.
4. "Isn't this FUN?" chirped Trina for the tenth time in five minutes, causing the others to roll their eyes while they continued digging the SUV out of the mud.
5. Marvin blushes when others talk to him and won't even look at himself in the mirror.
6. After ten minutes of screaming and putting coats over their heads during *Possible Side Effects*, half the audience members wound up sitting in the lobby, waiting for the movie to end.
7. Whatever Skeeter wears, the other guys wear.
8. "What?! *Your* dog doesn't do karaoke like *mine*?" asked Valerie.
9. The sweat began puddling on desks even before Professor Linchpin passed out the chemistry final.
10. The principal's eyes were icy, and his voice was even icier as he confronted those responsible for the the food-coloring-in-the-fountain incident.

Avoid Bloat by Eliminating Word Overdose
Page 20, Practice

1. After his special training, Sylvester could hypnotize sheep and was an expert at it before the unfortunate incident with a ram.

2. At the reading of her Uncle Lester's will, Miss Primpton learned that she inherited his 729 piece collection of porcelain rodents.

3. Miss Primpton was not at all pleased about receiving the porcelain rodents because she was really hoping to inherit the button factory.

4. Mom knows that because teen fashion fads don't last, she will not have to put up with Stella's "gutter creature" fashion statement for long. Soon Stella will have a new look she will hate.

5. Now Adelaide thinks her cake will win the Cakes Based on Great Literature competition because nobody has yet constructed the house in *The House of Seven Gables* out of spice cake, cinnamon sticks, and Necco wafers.

6. Randolph and Priscilla hope to win first prize in the Cakes Based on Great Literature competition. If they win, it will be because their triple layer presentation of Edgar Allan Poe's "The Masque of the Red Death" stunned the judges.

Build Strong Sentences with Powerful Verbs
Page 22, Practice #1

1. The ogre *sneaked* up behind the troll and bopped him a good one for the tar and feather prank he'd pulled two weeks ago.

2. Mrs. Freytag *raced* to the back of the classroom when Bobby tipped over the ant farm.

3. Deep inside, Hazelton *despised* inspecting asphalt for a living.

4. "But why can't I have another piece of pear pie?" Petunia *pouted*.

5. When the principal *bellowed* over the intercom that he wanted to see Walter in his office immediately, we suspected it was Walter who painted the extra arrows on the parking lot.

6. "And just why," Mom *yelled*, "are we finding it necessary to dye the dog's hair in the living room?"

7. Fred *grabbed* his things and left the scene of the bouncing UFO.

Page 22, Practice #2

1. "No!" shrieked Ms. Massey, as she noted the impressive pile of sugar, flour, and coffee little Maxwell managed to dump onto the kitchen floor in the fifteen minutes he was alone in the kitchen.

2. "Petey and Joey, march downstairs right now!" sputtered Ms. Massey, after one of the neighbors called to tell her the boys had written "Help! We're bein' held prizners!" on the back of the upstairs window shade.

3. Numerous small footprints zigzagged down the fresh sidewalk cement, convincing Ms. Massey that a vacation—all by herself—was long overdue.

Lose the Ho-Hum by Using Vivid Metaphors
Page 24, Practice #1

1. The team was a herd of bison rumbling onto the football field.

2. Her dress is a sunset of pink and orange and yellow.

3. Stewart is having a hangnail kind of day.
4. As far as Winifred is concerned, math story problems are the tsunamis of any school day.
5. After Celia dumped him, Pedro's heart was a deflated balloon.
6. After their "Extreme Polka" class, Andy and Beverly were a couple of flat Cokes with no fizz left.

Page 24, Practice #2

1. If you ask me, Lea's whiny little poodle is a maddening drip, drip, drip from the faucet in the middle of the night.
2. Licorice jelly beans are the caviar of the candy world.
3. In Aunt Olive's opinion, heavy metal is a sandblaster for the eardrums.

Revive These Sentences, Review #3
Page 25, Show Instead of Tell

1. "*Evening of Enchantment* smells like a bouquet of flowers," noted Mimi, after sampling several bottles of perfume at the store counter, "but *Possibilities* smells like buffalo droppings—in my opinion."
2. When Mr. Chartreuse got that funny squeak in his voice and his eye started to twitch, we knew the bell curve just turned upside down.

Page 25, Avoid Word Overdose

1. Helen soon found out that the cake tasted odd *because* her little brother Frankie added toothpaste to the batter when she wasn't looking.
2. The magician included a refrigerator *and* a llama in his disappearing act *because* it would impress the audience.

Page 26, Use Powerful Verbs

1. Sammy swore he was *tiptoeing* past the toothpick sculptures from the Around the World display when suddenly all 5,297 toothpicks in the Eiffel Tower replica tipped over and fell on top of the miniature Taj Mahal.
2. Sammy also *insisted* that he was just standing at a slight angle to get a better look at the Sand Sculptures of Historic Events when he suddenly fell right into the middle of "The French Revolution."
3. For the rest of the field trip through the Winchester W. Threadbare Art Museum, Principal Wiggins *shadowed* Sammy to make sure there were no more "accidents" involving statues.

Page 26, Use Vivid Metaphors

1. The extreme chili-dog eating contest winner's stomach is a bottomless cast-iron cauldron.
2. To little Timmy, the shadows on the wall were dancing acrobats tumbling along the floor and swinging and leaping through the trees.

Revive These Sentences, Review #4
Page 27, Show Instead of Tell

1. Besides suffering the consequences of a corn dog that was apparently long past its freshness date, Abby lost her flip-flops high atop the Ferris wheel.
2. Ned laughed himself silly over the skate-boarding baboon on YouTube.

Page 27, Avoid Word Overdose

1. If part "Y" does not fit easily into part "Z," you may have inserted the zimwats incorrectly. Before reassembling, remove the zimwats by pulling on Tab X.
2. After her retirement from the Q-Tip factory, Aunt Vesta took up bungee jumping and now loves her new sport.

Page 27, Use Powerful Verbs

1. Bob and Joe celebrated when they finally got permission to open up a Bait and Smoothie kiosk on the pier.
2. When we finally got there, Dad howled upon seeing that he had forgotten to put the lid on the paint can in the trunk of the car.

Page 27, Use Vivid Metaphors

1. After Clarise told him to hit the road, Chaz was a leaking jug of tears.
2. Leonora is a firecracker waiting to explode over Craig forgetting the second anniversary of their first date on the Fourth of July.

Lose Choppiness with Compound Sentences
Page 32, Practice

Geraldine was trying to remember which clown she hired for Sonny's birthday party. She wanted to hire the same one for Minnie's party. Was it Giggles the Clown, or was it Mr. Bubblehead? Maybe it was Mr. Sniffles, or maybe it was Jiggles the Jester. It could have been Mr. Velcro or even Bobo the Hobo. She just couldn't remember, so she decided to call the clown agency.

For Added Pep, Use Prepositional Phrases
Page 35, Practice

1. The *Supermarket Tattler* reports that Bigfoot often appears (in the back) (of the semi truck) (behind the snack food warehouse).
2. Anna, however, was quite sure she saw Bigfoot (on top) (of the Henderson's barn) (on Wednesday) (after the homecoming dance).
3. Harrison claimed he saw a flying cement truck (near the sewage treatment plant) (at the edge) (of town).
4. "The lawn mower's (in the living room) (by the grand piano)," hollered Max.
5. Stuart strapped on his gravity boots (during his presentation) (at the science fair).

Page 35, Challenge

1. Harrison claims he saw a giant groundhog (in the grocery store) (by the canned creamed corn display).
2. We're a little worried (about Harrison).
3. Max keeps a year's supply (of Oreos) (in the living room).
4. After Anna claimed that she saw Bigfoot (on top) (of the Henderson's barn), she admitted that she was not wearing her glasses (on that particular evening).
5. (Without her glasses), Anna often sees things that are invisible (to others).

Add Life to Anemic Sentences with Appositives
Page 37, Practice #1

1. Otis really liked the Tuesday lunch special, the "Gut-Buster Chili Dog," at the Gonzo Burger Café.
2. Our dog, a miniature poodle called Hugo the Magnificent, got loose in the petting zoo.
3. The first time I saw Great Uncle Arbuthnot's house, the one with fifteen life-sized plastic gnomes in the front yard, I understood why we hardly ever go there.
4. Memory expert Elmo Doorknob, a man famous for remembering all the words to the U.S. Constitution, claimed he just "forgot" to pay his taxes all those years.
5. Buford, the seventh grader who recited "The Charge of the Light Brigade" backwards in sixty seconds, won first prize in the school's "Unusual Talents" competition.

Page 37, Practice #2

1. Out of everything that happened to our dog when he got loose in the petting zoo, I think the stare-down with Thelma, the miniature cow with an attitude, was the funniest.
2. Stanley, the talking elephant that keeps showing up in Benson's dreams, gives Benson valuable advice about attracting girls.
3. On his front lawn, Great Uncle Arbuthnot has several old sofas, sofas that clearly have been there for many years.

Liven Up These Ho-Hum Sentences, Review #5
Pages 38-39

1. Shelley, the world's best nose flute player, came in second in the school's "Unusual Talents" competition.
2. Hans was pretty sure the skunk was hiding under the lace tablecloth in his grandmother's linen closet.
3. Great Aunt Azalea is coming to visit and wants to bring her pets, two obnoxious and ill-behaved standard poodles.
4. Mitzy broke the zipper on her Dora the Explorer backpack, but she wasn't worried about it.
5. It was cold outside, so Mrs. Nantucket, a woman who takes spoiling to new heights, put a sweater on her Chihuahua.
6. Today Jillian added two more characters, Miss Piggy and Ariel, to her "favorite cartoon characters" quilt.
7. Presley explained how to get to the snake zoo with 979 boa constrictors on display in the center of town.
8. The Wriggling Family Jugglers, the most accident-prone team in circus history, just added two more items to their list of unusual things to juggle.
9. Gretel ordered a dish of Wicked Watermelon ice cream with hot fudge sauce, and she ordered some sprinkles to put on top.
10. Grady had a hard time getting the stuffed frog out of the dryer vent and into the box on the floor.

Liven Up These Ho-Hum Sentences, Review #6
Pages 40-41

1. My dog Woofer, who is quite fastidious, wears sunglasses in the sun, and when it rains he wears boots. (Created a compound sentence and added an appositive)

2. Sal chased the hedgehog through the courtyard, around the fence, and right into the compost heap. (Added three prepositional phrases)

3. Thelma enjoys making peach pies for senior citizen pot lucks, but she would rather track big game. (Added a prepositional phrase and created a compound sentence)

4. Ned won the yodeling contest, but many thought that Nita would have won if she hadn't inhaled a gnat during her performance. (Created a compound sentence and added a prepositional phrase)

5. Abe, the man who submitted several potatoes that resemble the faces of famous people, won second prize in the unusual vegetable contest, and Claire won third prize for her polka-dotted beets. (Created a compound sentence, added an appositive and a prepositional phrase)

6. Princess Peony finally saw Finnigan when he rescued her from the Tower for Keeping Marriageable Princesses from Eligible Princes until All the Dragons are Slain. (Added prepositional phrases)

7. Our English teacher told us that we should learn how to write compound sentences, and then she will reward us with gummy bears. (Added a prepositional phrase and created a compound sentence)

Page 41, Bonus

- Compound sentence: Lionel won the yodeling contest, but he lost the final round.
- Sentence with prepositional phrases: To supplement her income, our English teacher proofreads "possible side effects" lists for pharmaceutical companies, and she plays Bingo on Friday nights.
- Compound sentence with prepositional phrases: To make sure he had rid the kingdom of all dragons, Prince Finnigan checked behind the castle, inside the moat, and all around the Forest of Fearsome Beasts, but just to make sure, he also checked his Dragon GPS.
- Sentence with an appositive: Princess Peony, a woman tired of waiting for a prince, decided to open up a "really sparkly jewelry" boutique.
- Compound sentence with prepositional phrases and an appositive: Thelma's most recent trip, a safari to a big game preserve in Africa, was thrilling, so she decided to open up a business arranging safaris for seniors.

Connect with Pairs of Conjunctions
Page 43, Practice #1

1. My dentist plans on entering either his "denture seconds" collection or his "rocks-that-look-like-molars" collection in the U.S. Dental Goodies Fair.

2. According to what I've heard, both Ms. Blair and Ms. Rizzuto are known for remembering all the rules for commas, though they tend to put students to sleep when they talk about them.

3. Neither Grandpa nor Uncle Louie cares for Aunt Janine's mashed yam and broccoli pie.

Page 43, Practice #2

1. Neither Jake nor his brother liked eating cereal without sugar, but their mother would buy only Sugar-free Wheat Bombs for breakfast.

2. They not only hate Sugar-free Wheat Bombs but also the soy milk she serves with it.

Cure the Blahs with Participial Phrases
Page 45, Practice #1

1. Noting the approach of the green slimy thing with three eyes and large pointy teeth, Jed decided to back out of the swamp.

2. Having just learned that he gave up riding wild boars just for her, Talula swore she would love Ansel—and only Ansel—forever.

Page 45, Practice #2

1. The baby laughed and then started to hiccup, causing the parrot to chirp, "Uh-oh!"
2. Harry was pretty sure that kid was the one who spray-painted his lawn purple, ruining his chances of winning the best lawn competition this year.

Page 45, Practice #3

1. Ms. Flindersniddle, savoring the success of the Semi-Colon Scavenger Hunt, smiled when she found out the Comma Derby was the final competition in the Pan-Pacific Punctuation Games.
2. Quotation Mark Marathon champion Spencer Fontleroy, realizing he has only one more opportunity to earn the coveted Golden Exclamation Mark for most wins in the Pan-Pacific Punctuation Games, hopes to make it to the sudden death playoffs in the Hyphen Match.

Page 45, Practice #4

1. Eddie smiled as he typed in a semi-colon, knowing that the punctuation mark he had chosen would likely boost him over the top in number of points earned.
2. The judge for the competition looked at the results, frowning with disapproval at the name at the top of the list.

Add Oomph with Relative Clauses
Page 47, Practice

1. The kid with the purple hair is the one who made pretzels shaped like bugs to enter in the annual cooking class "Snack Off" competition.
2. Syd, who is the newest member of the country-punk band Psycho Billy, plays the electric harp.
3. Artist Renfro P. Sledgehammer is the award-winning sculptor of the five-ton granite nose that sits outside the ear, nose, and throat clinic and attracts all the pigeons.
4. The bank robber, who absentmindedly took a bite out of his licorice gun while he was waiting for the cashier to hand over the money, also used one of the security mirrors to adjust his fake mustache.
5. Besides working as a knife-thrower's assistant before she became a best-selling author, Allison Cantaloupe was the high-wire juggler who used an assortment of vegetables and paring knives for her performance.

Page 47, Challenge

1. All students whose last names begin with X should report to the office immediately.
2. A sudden loss of hair and nails that occurs after using Kazam! Instant Tooth Brightener should be reported to your doctor immediately.
3. The concert, which sold out in five minutes, featured Jane's favorite group: Pete Moss and the Electric Bagpipe Quintet.

Bring These Incomplete Sentences To Life, Review #7
Page 48, Pairs of conjunctions

1. Cal decided to both transmit FM radio stations through his dental fillings and spin on his big toe in the *Earth's Got Talent* Competition.
2. Henrietta was surprised to find not only her shoes but also her biology text book when she opened the refrigerator door.

Page 48, Participial Phrases

1. Looking out the window before his party, Jose saw a porcupine scurrying around the backyard popping all the birthday balloons.
2. Mr. Bobblehead tried to look innocent, bobbing up and down in the police line-up.
3. Seeing a cloud of foamy white stuff billowing toward him, D.J. ran as fast as he could from the exploding marshmallow factory.

Page 48, Relative Clauses

1. The winner of this year's hot tamale eating contest is Hector Waterfaucet, who downed 67 tamales and a quart of antacid.
2. Renee finally found the source of the smell that emptied the Bingo parlor in five minutes.

Page 48, Challenge

Knowing anything could happen on a mid-town subway in September, neither Spike, who sat in the front seat, nor Carmine, who sat next to him, was surprised when three whistling Easter bunnies climbed aboard.

Bring These Incomplete Sentences To Life, Review #8
Page 49, Pairs of Conjunctions

1. Chloe, known for her off-beat sense of style, wasn't sure what to wear to the safari-themed dance. She was considering either the leopard-print tutu with the fur jacket or the fringed leather cape over the zebra-print body suit.
2. Little Will was going through a phase where he would only eat yellow-colored food. Both wax bean soup and creamed corn were on the list of his preferred foods at that time.
3. Carlton has unusual pets. He has raised not only three lemurs but also six arachnids and one crustacean—but not at the same time.

Pages 49-50, Participial Phrases

1. Heloise saw the hairy bug her brother told her about. We knew she found it when, screaming and running around in circles, she kept pointing to her backpack.
2. From lighting cheeseburger-scented candles to munching purple popcorn, Nelly has found several unusual ways to help her study for tests. Wearing a bathing suit at her desk, she finds that the chill helps keep her awake.
3. The last time Brewster was in a fancy gift shop he tipped over a display of glass toads. Stumbling over the broken toads, he then knocked over a shelf full of glass bumblebees.

Page 50, Relative Clauses

1. Concert pianist Niles Flamingo, who plays the piano very fast, recently performed the "Minute Waltz" in 50 seconds.
2. We finally figured out that the stuff that was moving in the container in the bottom of the refrigerator was the long-forgotten fish and eggplant casserole.
3. Francine got her hair dyed the day before her wedding by a new stylist, who accidentally put a little too much red in the mix.

Add Interest with Subordinate Clauses
Page 52, Practice

1. Our cat Mr. Noodles hates to have his toenails clipped unless there's a little catnip involved.
2. Boomer's favorite paint names to date include "Rusted Tin," "Dirt," and "WD-40," although he's just come up with another he likes: "Turpentine."
3. Zippy the Amazing Beetle is Dad's favorite racing beetle since Scuttles retired.
4. Horton suggested filling the swamp with tapioca pudding because nobody had come up with anything the boss liked so far.
5. Amelia is a longtime fan of the metal band Hammer & Nails, although she also really likes listening to reruns of the old Lawrence Welk show.

Add Punch Now and Then with Short Sentences
Page 54, Practice

1. Although electric zithers are gaining popularity among indy punkers, they were first used in the garage band Painted Toenails in 1968. Or so we hear. The Toenails' lead guitarist "Ty Dye" (Quenton Smythers, originally from Eugene, Oregon, now an insurance salesman in Toledo) is modest about his influence, however.
2. Excited about winning first place at this year's Yarn Spinners' Knit-off, my mother has decided to knit Noah's Ark, animals included, for next year's competition. She is in the process of selecting which animal pairs to include. Besides the usuals, she thinks the addition of alpacas, otters, and wombats ought to impress the judges. At least she hopes so.
3. The International Thumb Wrestling Federation is having its next championship meet in Drain, Oregon. Yes, "Drain." Thumb wrestling enthusiasts from all over the world are expected to attend this three day event. Drain beat Boring, Oregon, in a fierce battle to host the event. Yes, "Boring."
4. We just found out that cousins Otis and Bo are coming for the holidays again, and Mom is not happy. After they left last year she found gobs of used gum stuck underneath the kitchen chairs. The boys didn't bathe for a week, they ate like pigs, and they had armpit burping contests. Mom's thinking of moving and not leaving a forwarding address. Do you blame her?
5. Glick, Lord Hemisphere's sidekick/slave was feeling especially unappreciated. It was hard being at His Lordship's beck and call all the time. It was annoying to hear, "Glick, do this," and "Glick, do that," day in and day out. In short, Glick was fed up with slavery. Was it too much to ask, he wondered, for a weekend off now and then to relax at the Boar's Head Inn or hunt dragons? Absolutely not.

Keep Things Nicely Balanced with Parallelism
Page 56, Practice #1

1. Beginning power tool jugglers are prone to crying, screaming, and quitting.
2. WARNING: Before assembling your very own nuclear submarine, be sure to update your will, warn your neighbors, and don your lead underwear.
3. Benson found another ointment to try on his rash but decided against that one, too, when he read about its possible side effects: rattling vocal cords, curling fingernails, and vibrating intestines.

Pages 56-57, Practice #2

1. Our hamster Twitch is so obsessed with his hamster ball he would roll around the house all morning, all afternoon, and all night if we let him.
2. According to the latest issue of the *Supermarket Tattler*, the Ammonia People from Neptune are the ones hiding Elvis, making banjo patterns in corn fields, and trying to get in touch with Big Foot.
3. Leroy's favorite Golden Boot Award country bands are the 2002 winner Outta Luck, the 2004 winner Bad Habits, and the 2008 winner, the Abner Hooligan Jug Band.
4. Legend has it that Igor of the ancient Fo-fum Clan whomped the ogre, beaned the troll, and kicked the gnome.
5. Benson was considering the ointment for his rash until he learned that possible side effects included spontaneous boils, irritable liver, and exploding gall bladder.
6. "To get to the castle," began the gnome, "you must slog through the stinking swamp, ascend the slimy steps, and thrash through the thistly thicket."

Inject Some Energy into These Sentences, Review #9
Page 58, Subordinate Clauses

1. Demi agreed to take her little brother and his friends to see *Night of the Rattlesnakes, 3-D*, if they finish their popcorn and sodas before the part where the snakes devour the campers.
2. "Listen, Cyd," whispered Leon, "I think the giant chicken saw us. Be careful when you take off your feather suit."
3. Although she is taking fewer risks since last year's bungee jumping episode, Grandma agreed to ride the "Rollercoaster Scream Express" with Ryan, just this once.
4. Smedley preferred expensive cologne, Italian shoes, Mister Swell suits, and caviar, whereas Slick preferred the smell of diesel exhaust, hip boots, coveralls, and Cousin Curly's five-alarm chili.
5. Since Jack chose travelling the mud wrestling circuit over his relationship with Mindy, Mindy has been sighing a thousand sighs, crying a thousand tears, and throwing darts at his picture.

Page 59, Short Sentences

Jeb's Tips on How to Succeed in School, Part 1

- Come prepared for class with all the books and other tools necessary to do your best. Arrange everything neatly in front of you so that you are prepared to perform any task required. Power down all cell phones, iPods, iPhones, MP3 players, beepers, buzzers, flashers, blinkers, and any other gadgets that might distract you and everyone else and cause your teacher to give you even more looks you don't want. Avoid the "disintegrater stare."

- Show respect to all school staff including teachers, guidance counselors, secretaries, attendance clerks, maintenance technicians, and crossing guards. Do not address them with terms like "Yo," "Hey," "Teach," or "Dude." Especially don't say, "Babe." Instead call them by their names preceded by a title ("Mr. Sparkplug," "Principal Vanderhoovenflindernoggin," "Sister Angelica").

Page 59, Parallelism

1. The three main ingredients in Cousin Curly's five-alarm chili are red hot peppers, green hot peppers, and white hot peppers.
2. We're pretty sure the iguana is hiding inside the heat register, behind the shower stall, or underneath Patsy's pile of clothes in the corner.
3. Before assembling your new piano, arrange all 1,479 pieces, line up your wrenches, and clean your tuning fork.
4. So far, Aunt Germaine's All-Purpose Cream has been found helpful for dry skin, clogged sinks, and rusty carburetors.

Inject Some Energy into These Sentences, Review #10
Page 60, Subordinate Clauses

1. Mark insisted on wearing his Superman costume to school because he had a strong feeling he might have to save the city that very day.
2. Ray's favorite meal was salad, meatloaf, mashed potatoes, and apple pie, whereas Poncho liked cheese puffs and root beer.
3. "Okay, you can go to the flea market," said Mom, "as long as you don't bring home any fleas."

Page 60, Short Sentences

First, Bridget tied the little pink bib with the rosebud print around Suzie's neck. Next, she gently pulled on two pairs of little white ruffled socks and then carefully fitted a lace bonnet on Suzie's head. Perfect! But just as Bridget started to put the matching lace shawl around Suzie's shoulders, the bulldog woke up, sniffed at her strange outfit, and ran straight for a mud puddle.

Page 60, Parallelism

1. Sasha's collections of bottles of ketchup from Nebraska truck stops, tubes of toothpaste from around the world, and chunks of asphalt from major interstates won her first prize in the Unusual Collections Competition.
2. Raul watched as the man in the mattress suit advertising a sale at Mattress City danced, twirled, and somersaulted on the street corner.

Connect with Conjunctive Adverbs
Page 62, Practice #1

1. "I'm particularly receptive to compliments today," said Lilly; still, Chip went on with the engine overhaul.
2. Aurillia decided against joining Future Game Show Hosts of America. Instead, she took up the tuba.
3. In the crime scene investigative drama *CSI North Dakota*, bad guy Lenny the Lip was replaced by Joey Carburetor; nevertheless, ratings stalled.

Page 62, Practice #2

1. Uncle Harvey loves Mom's "Black and Blue Casserole," which features black cumin and blue fenugreek; however, that dish makes my little brother throw up.

2. Spices starting with the letter "C" make my brother sneeze. Consequently, he has a bad reaction to Mom's chive and chili chimichangas.

3. The dishes my little brother does like are usually seasoned with "L" spices like licorice, lime, and lemon; however, he has never met an "O" spice he doesn't like.

Page 62, Practice #3

1. Uncle Harvey considers himself a bit of a gourmet cook. However, after the Flaming Turtle Chocolate Fondue incident, we encourage him to bring only non-flammable gourmet food to our potlucks.

2. Jeb and Hortense are unaware of the drain pipes silently but relentlessly eroding under the kitchen sink; consequently, the couple will soon be in for a big surprise.

3. Anson has decided to change careers. He feels he's been collecting money for the Internal Revenue Service long enough; instead, he'd like to herd cattle.

Add Interest with Infinitive Phrases
Page 63, Practice #1

1. To find out if Spot was actually the one eating all the Fig Newtons stored in the cupboard above the sink, the dog's owner installed a video camera in the kitchen.

2. To see if there was really a miniature llama in their new neighbors' back yard, Mallory and Chuck looked out the back window.

3. To get to the Inter-Planetary Food Critics Convention on time, Boris and Elrod took Galactic Express # 9.

4. To understand what the little space dude was saying, Betty got out her electronic translator.

Page 64, Practice #2

1. To figure out how to make it stop sparking and smoking, Lemuel turned to page 127 of the instruction manual for his new Whizmadoodle.

2. To get to the top of Mount Many Annoying Loose Rocks (as the locals called it), the explorer had to ride a goat.

3. To help raise money for the yarn factory, the sheep herders organized a tamale feed.

4. To make a cake for the snorkelers' club fund raiser, Edna needed six more sacks of flour, two more sacks of sugar, five dozen eggs, a quart of blue food coloring, and a really big pan.

5. To win the International Toughest Guy competition, Barney was prepared to climb the highest mountains, swim the most treacherous rivers, ride the roughest roads, lift the heaviest weights, and even single-handedly chaperone a bus load of six-year-olds to and from a field trip to the candy factory.

Page 64, Practice #3

1. To get the elephant to settle down, the new animal trainer sang him lullabies.

2. To lead her group back from the wilderness, the lost tour guide followed animal tracks until she came to a 7-11.

3. To silence the giggling girls, the irritated librarian gave them some gum.

4. To calm his fears once and for all before his first big presentation, the nervous public speaker started imagining all the audience members in Easter bunny costumes.

Page 64, Practice #4

To fool her brother into trying her spinach cheesecake, Edna frosted it with chocolate icing.

Time to Practice, Review #11
Page 65, Conjunctive Adverbs

1. Jill has so far saved only $14.98 toward the $50,000 she needs to open a potato chip factory; still, she will pursue her dream.

2. Having just found out she is allergic to lions, Loretta turned down the job offer with the circus; instead, she accepted a position teaching middle school English.

3. After years of musical training on several instruments, Greg decided to join a rock and roll band. However, there didn't seem to be much call for flugelhorn players, bassoonists, or harpists.

Page 65, Infinitive Phrases

1. To frighten the neighborhood children, Mr. Jones dressed up like a math story problem teacher last Halloween.

2. To calm them down, the camp counselor assured the little campers that there were no gorillas waiting for them behind the outhouse.

Page 65, Challenge

To darken the newscaster's eyebrows, the new makeup girl, a little nervous, accidentally used black nail polish; consequently, his eyebrows were shiny and immovable for a very long time.

Time to Practice, Review #12
Page 66, Conjunctive Adverbs

1. Just as little Libby came to understand the gurgle-uck-duk-duk-duk-duk sound at night was the refrigerator itself and not a monster within, she became aware of other sounds that made her lie awake in the dark for hours; therefore, her mother had to send her to a sleep therapist.

2. Reactions to the boil ointment may include vertigo, clown hallucinations, and swollen knee caps; consequently, it is not a good idea to use it if you develop these symptoms.

Page 66, Infinitive Phrases

1. To improve his luncheon special, Carleton added a dash of pepper, a pinch of salt, and a can of sardines.

2. To prepare to open your new Ajax Build-It-Yourself-Rocket, make sure your garage is well ventilated and you have a few boxes of earplugs and a case or two of Band-aids.

Page 66, Challenge

To add interest to his garlic mashed potatoes, Carleton molded them into the shape of a bunny; consequently, little Bianca wouldn't touch them.

Practice Adding Life to More Yawners, Review #13
Page 67, Yawner #1

Cousin Dizzy and the Polka Renegades got stuck in traffic. The traffic report said the gridlock could last an hour or more because a semitruck full of strawberries had tipped over. The Renegades were already late for rehearsal, so they decided to rehearse right there on the interstate. Channel 9 news reported later that Cousin Dizzy and the boys gave new meaning to the phrase "traffic jam."

Page 67, Yawner #2

It was Zippy the Amazing Beetle's first race, and he was racing against the dreaded Beetle Mania. Standing thorax to thorax, they waited for the sound of the pop gun that started the race. Bang! Beetle Mania zoomed past Zippy in the first lap. Then he got stuck in a gum wad on the track. Zippy scuttled past Beetle Mania and sped ahead while Beetle Mania pried himself loose. Free at last, he sped up behind Zippy. He wasn't fast enough, though, and Zippy won by a feeler.

Page 67, Yawner #3

The knitting competition was fierce. My mom thought her knitted "Noah's Ark Tableau" would win first place, but she saw that Imelda Renoir's "Taj Mahal Replica" was good, too. That creation included 103 miniature tourists and six tour busses, which were very impressive. Mom was not dismayed, however. She figured her last minute addition of 27 extinct species on the Ark would at least get her the award for knitting projects promoting environmental awareness.

Page 67, Yawner #4

My little brother, who has unusual interests, likes to glue things together. He considers his miniature space lab made of packing peanuts, bottle caps, sticks, and empty milk cartons to be his best effort to date. He's pretty excited about his current project. He's building a G.I. Joe fort out of Mom's pots and pans while she's busy in the basement cleaning up the mess made by the storm. He won't be excited for long, though.

Page 67, Yawner #5

Little Libby got a new doll, the kind that talks. To save money, her parents got it at the factory seconds outlet. They soon discovered why it was a "second," though. Instead of "I love you, Mommy," the doll said things like, "Die, aliens!" and "Off with their heads!"

Practice Adding Life to More Yawners, Review #14
Page 68, Yawner #1

Dear Jim,

I've lost Mr. Bazooka! Have you seen him anywhere? After the accident he looks more like a cross between a rat and a chipmunk than a dog. You'll know it's him because he can do tricks. If you whistle once, he will stand on his hind legs. If you whistle twice, he will stand on his hind legs and spin, and if you whistle three times, he will fall over. Or that might be because he's dizzy. Anyway, he eats only liver kibbles and rhubarb, and to get him to come to you just yodel any tune on "Kenny The Yodeling Mailman's Greatest Hits" CD.

B.J.

Page 68, Yawner #2

To: Discount Realtors

From: The Smiths

Re: The house for sale on 8th Avenue

We're afraid the "cozy handyman's dream" we looked at on 8th Avenue isn't quite what we want. We were hoping for something larger with at least one inside bathroom. We were expecting the "bonus room" in the basement to have a floor, four complete walls, and no vermin. We were also concerned about the stench wafting out of the fireplace and the 152 holes in the "pocket-sized" back yard. The place definitely lives up to its billing as a "unique" fixer-upper; however, I'm afraid its not for us.

Sincerely,

The Smiths

Page 68, Yawner #3

Watching the Battle of the Bands contest at the fairgrounds, it was easy to see why The Jeeter Crabtree Kazoo Ensemble won the "most original band" award. Who knew seven kazoo players could produce so many musical styles, everything from Bach to the Grateful Dead? Their costumes were also original, although I would think that so many feathers might cause a sneezing hazard. And their special effects were amazing, especially the fireworks synchronized with the theme songs to 1950s television shows.

About the author

Phyllis Beveridge Nissila is an award-winning former humor columnist who has taught middle school, high school, and community college classes for over twenty years. She is currently teaching adult basic education classes at Lane Community College in Eugene, Oregon, as well as private literature and writing classes for home schooled students.

MORE GREAT BOOKS FROM COTTONWOOD PRESS

UNJOURNALING—Daily Writing exercises That Are NOT Personal, NOT Introspective, NOT Boring! The more than 200 impersonal but engaging writing prompts in this exercise book help students practice their writing skills without asking them to share personal thoughts they would rather keep to themselves.

A SENTENCE A DAY—Short, playful proofreading exercises to help students avoid tripping up when they write. This book focuses on short, playful, interesting sentences with a sense of humor.

ATTITUDE!—Helping students WANT to succeed in school and then setting them up for success. Pointing out what school has to do with real life, this easy-to-use book is enlightening and never preachy.

DOWNWRITE FUNNY—Using student's love of the ridiculous to build serious writing skills. The entertaining activities and illustrations in this book help teach all kinds of useful writing skills.

HOT FUDGE MONDAY—Tasty Ways to Teach Parts of Speech to Students Who Have a Hard Time Swallowing Anything To Do With Grammar. This new edition includes quirky quizzes, extended writing activities, and Internet enrichment activities that reinforce new skills.

THINKING IN THREES—The Power of Three in Writing. Faced with a writing task of any kind? Think of three things to say about the topic. Writing an essay? Remember that the body should have at least three paragraphs. Need help getting started? Learn three ways to begin an essay.

IF THEY'RE LAUGHING THEY JUST MIGHT BE LISTENING—Ideas for using HUMOR effectively in the classroom—even if you're NOT funny yourself. Discover ways to lighten up, encourage humor from others, and have fun with your students.

RELUCTANT DISCIPLINARIAN—Advice on classroom management from a softy who became (eventually) a successful teacher. Author Gary Rubinstein offers clear and specific advice for classroom management.

HOW TO HANDLE DIFFICULT PARENTS—A teacher's survival guide. Suzanne Capek Tingley identifies characteristics of some parent "types". She then goes on to give practical, easy-to-implement methods of working with them more effectively.

TWISTING ARMS—Teaching students how to write to persuade. This book is full of easy-to-use activities that will really sharpen students' writing and organizational skills.

COTTONWOOD PRESS INC.
www.cottonwoodpress.com